A Business History of Soy

This is a business history of soy that reveals how Japanese imperial and military institutions and financial–mercantile–industrial interests created a role for soy as a versatile raw material and global commodity beginning in the 19th century, even before the Western world recognized this "oilseed." Originating in the rich food cultures of Asia, soy is praised as the "magic bean." About 360 million tons are produced in the world today, and it is traded globally to become food, feed, and fuel. It is the second largest source of vegetable oil in the world, and soy meal is an essential feed without which the modern livestock industries could not exist. Its dominance today is often accounted for in terms of its versatile nature. This book, however, argues that soy was transformed into a versatile industrial raw material and global commodity through the political-economic strategies of state and business actors engaged in the development of the capitalist world-economy. By studying little-known Japanese historical documents and corporate records, and focusing on the less-researched vegetable oil and industrial uses of soy, this book provides a better understanding of how this traditional Asian food was transformed into a global commodity embedded in contradictions. Promoted as a healthy and sustainable food source, soy is also a destructive cash crop whose cultivation and use have played a significant role in the current climate crisis. Based on this case of soy, the book provides a structural understanding of broader food and agriculture systems in the history of capitalism, making it of interest to students at an advanced level, academics, and researchers in the fields of business history, corporate governance, Japanese business, as well as the political economy of food and agriculture.

Midori Hiraga is an associate professor in the Faculty of Economics at Kyoto Tachibana University, Japan.

Routledge International Studies in Business History
Series editors: Heidi Tworek and Ai Hisano

Industrial Clusters
Knowledge, Innovation Systems and Sustainability in the UK
Edited by John F. Wilson, Chris Corker and Joe Lane

Postcolonial Transition and Global Business History
British Multinational Companies in Ghana and Nigeria
Stephanie Decker

The Rise of Digital Management
From Industrial Mobilization to Platform Capitalism
François-Xavier de Vaujany

A History of the Aviation Industry in Latin America
Nationalism, Developmentalism and Neoliberalism in Chile
Diego Barría Traverso

A Business History of Retail
From Trading Post to E-commerce in America and Canada
Bettina Liverant

A Business History of Latin America
Edited by Andrea Lluch, Martín Monsalve Zanatti and Marcelo Bucheli

A Business History of Soy
Japan's Modernization and the Rise of Soy as a Global Commodity
Midori Hiraga

For more information about this series, please visit: www.routledge.com/Routledge-International-Studies-in-Business-History/book-series/SE0471

A Business History of Soy

Japan's Modernization and the Rise of Soy as a Global Commodity

Midori Hiraga

Routledge
Taylor & Francis Group
NEW YORK AND LONDON

First published 2025
by Routledge
605 Third Avenue, New York, NY 10158

and by Routledge
4 Park Square, Milton Park, Abingdon, Oxon, OX14 4RN

Routledge is an imprint of the Taylor & Francis Group, an informa business

Library of Congress Cataloging-in-Publication Data
Names: Hiraga, Midori, author.
Title: A business history of soy : Japan's modernization and the rise of soy as a global commodity / Midori Hiraga.
Description: New York, NY : Routledge, 2025.
Series: Routledge international studies in business history |
Includes bibliographical references and index.
Identifiers: LCCN 2024029470 | ISBN 9781032673240 (hardback) |
ISBN 9781032678726 (paperback) | ISBN 9781032678733 (ebook)
Subjects: LCSH: Soybean industry–Japan–History. |
Soyfoods industry–Japan–History. | Japan–Commerce–History.
Classification: LCC HD9235.S62 J335 2025 |
DDC 338.1/73340952–dc23/eng/20240923
LC record available at https://lccn.loc.gov/2024029470

ISBN: 978-1-032-67324-0 (hbk)
ISBN: 978-1-032-67872-6 (pbk)
ISBN: 978-1-032-67873-3 (ebk)

DOI: 10.4324/9781032678733

Typeset in Galliard
by Newgen Publishing UK

The Open Access version of Chapters 2, 3 and the Conclusion was funded by Kyoto Tachibana University.

For Keith Addison,

who taught me the most

about this world.

1945–2014

R.I.P.

Contents

Figures

Tables

Note to the reader

Translation of Japanese materials:
Quotations from Japanese materials are translated into English by the author, including the direct quotations in double quote marks (" ").

Personal names:
Personal names in Japanese and Chinese are presented in the traditional fashion, with family name (in capital letters) followed by given name. The author did her best to accurately romanize names; however, Japanese names (written in Chinese characters) can have multiple readings, and the phonetic information is not always documented. I also consulted the Web NDL Authorities data created by the National Diet Library, Japan (https://id.ndl.go.jp/auth/ndla), for more accurate representation of Japanese authors' names.

Document and reference names:
When compiling the reference lists, the author translated Japanese book or document titles into English and also reproduced the original reference information in Japanese, instead of romanizing these titles.

For example, I provide the following reference:

Ooura, M. and Hirano, S. eds. (1948) *Golden Flower: The History of Japan Oil Company* (大浦万吉・平野茂之 編 [1948]『黄金の花: 日本製油株式会社沿革史（改訂増補版）』新潮社).

A romanized title (*Ogonnohana: Nihonseiyukabushikigaishaenkakushi*) is not included because it would carry little meaning for readers who do not understand Japanese, and provide confusing and defective information for those who do understand Japanese.

Corporate names:
Although the companies have changed their official corporate names and their organization structures over the past century-plus, to avoid confusion, this book uses one representative name for each company that developed from the same origin. For example, "Nisshin Soybean Crushing Co." became today's "Nisshin OilliO Group" after merging with several other companies, but this book calls it "Nisshin Oil" throughout, including in the reference information. Similarly, "Ajinomoto" is now used as a corporate name, but originally was the name of a product manufactured by a company named "Suzuki." Suzuki is a common family name in Japan, and this company has no relation to "Suzuki Shoten," the largest *zaibatsu* of Japan, which is mentioned frequently in this book. Thus, this book calls the former company "Ajinomoto" throughout, even when discussing the beginning of the business.

See the appendix for the basic corporate information and the current names and websites for the main companies discussed in this book.

Monetary values (yen):
All indications of monetary value in this book appear as written in the historical documents, and are thus the face value of the currency (mostly Japanese yen) in the period being discussed.

Weight units (tons):
This book refers to statistical data from various authors and agencies over a wide range of time. Many documents refer to the weight unit of a "ton" (in Japanese) without mentioning if it was a long tonne, a short ton, or a metric ton. The author translated all instances into English as "ton" unless otherwise specified in the original documents.

Introduction

Introduction: A business history of soy

Soy feeds the world and the global economy. According to the *Encyclopedia Britannica*, soy is "economically the most important bean in the world, providing vegetable protein for millions of people and ingredients for hundreds of chemical products" (2024). This book focuses on the business history of soy. Preceding the recognition of the bean by the Western world as now defined by the encyclopedia, this book reveals how the Japanese government and big business spearheaded the industrialization of soy, making it a versatile global commodity beginning in the 19th century. The main actors are Japanese oil companies and traders (later *sogo-shosha*), the financial-mercantile-industrial capital of *zaibatsu*, Japanese colonial institutions, the military, and the government. At the dawn of Japan's modernization, these business and political actors held strong reason for wanting to expand soy's usage and its markets, with little interest in food security. Its use at the time was mainly for non-food and military applications in the domestic context, and it was an export commodity which enabled Japan to accumulate capital and establish itself as a modern nation-state. They used soy as a convenient tool to strengthen their power to rapidly develop and catch up with the Western superpowers. Based on little-known Japanese historical documents and corporate records, this book aims to improve our fundamental understanding of how soy was transformed into a versatile commodity, coexisting within contradictory narratives: the façade of health and sustainable diets, while being synonymous with destructive agri-business practices, contributing significantly to today's climate and ecological crisis.

Around the end of the 19th century, Japan began to rapidly increase imports of soy from Manchuria.[1] The main purpose was not to fill people's stomachs but to use soy meal as fertilizer. Modernizing Japan needed fertilizer inputs to boost agricultural production, partly to grow food but mainly to increase silk production (which relies on cultivated mulberry leaf) for export to obtain foreign currency to finance the nation's industrial

DOI: 10.4324/9781032678733-1

development. The production of soy meal entails the production of soy oil, but the Japanese diet created very little demand for oil, so Japanese traders exported soy oil produced from Manchurian soy to the West, introducing soy to the world as a promising oilseed. Japanese business and political actors together developed the soy-industry and expanded the trade of soy products beyond Asia. This contributed to making Manchuria the global center of soy by the 1930s. These Japanese players made great efforts to create demand for their new products by expanding the uses of soy—beans, oil, and meal—as raw materials for non-food oleochemical and protein industries. Edible soy oil was an innovation that emerged from such Japanese companies' research and development projects, which led to new oil-based products entering the Japanese food market in the 1920s. When Japan stretched its battlefields across Asia and the Pacific in the 1930s and 1940s, soy became a precious resource for the petrol-lacking nation. The Japanese military ordered oil-related companies to develop various industrial and military products out of soy and other oilseeds, including lubricants, paints, glues, plastics, and glycerin for explosives. Only after WWII, and as a result of large-scale campaigns by both Japanese and US governments and businesses, did soy oil eventually become a daily foodstuff in the Japanese diet.

As an introduction to this business history of soy, this chapter first provides an overview of the current situation of soy and vegetable oils, along with related research. I then outline how the processes of soy's globalization and commodification have been studied to date, and explain why the Japanese case vividly demonstrates the fundamental transformation of soy at its very early stage. Lastly, I present the theoretical frameworks I use to study this transformation and how it occurred alongside the capitalist development of Japan.

Soy and vegetable oils: Current situation and related research

Soy as a global commodity

As a crucial global commodity, about 370 million metric tons of soy bean are produced annually in the world today. The Americas, led by the United States, Brazil, and Argentina, produce and export the most soy, accounting for about 87% of world production and 96% of soy exports. Asia was the native locality of soy, but today it is the largest regional importer, accounting for 76% of world imports. Among individual countries, China is the world's largest soy importer. Europe and Africa also require quite large amounts of soy (USDA 2023; FAOstat).

Oliveira and Hecht (2016, 2) point out the significant impacts of soy beyond food as below:

Table I.1 The production and trade of soy in the world in 2020 (unit: ton)

	Production	*Export quantity*	*Import quantity*
Americas	**308,025,177**	**167,136,649**	12,293,772
Asia	32,711,475	313,735	**127,580,015**
Europe	10,614,971	5,580,963	21,615,645
Africa	4,497,481	321,580	5,637,608
Oceania	17,323	1,028	7,329
World	355,866,427	173,353,955	167,134,370

Source: Compiled by the author based on the data from FAOstat Production, Food Balances (accessed January 6, 2024).

Note: Bold values are emphasis by the author.

> Soy is no simple staple crop—it is an agro-industrial feedstock, a complex assemblage of technologies and techniques for the flexible implementation of its production across highly variable landscapes, a global network of machinery, warehouses, trucks and ships channeling commodity flows to multiple markets around the world, structured by an even broader diversity of institutions, social relations and practices.

This dominance and dissemination of soy in the world was no natural phenomenon. It was the result of active human efforts over a century or two, strongly motivated by political and business strategies. In the introduction to their edited book, *World of Soy* (2008), Sidney W. Mintz, Chee-Beng Tan, and Christine M. Du Bois asserted that "hardly any other food plant is as modern as the soybean" (1), although Du Bois's later book, *The Story of Soy* (2018), presents 3,000 years of soy history beginning with its divine origins in ancient China. It is true that soy has been part of food culture for centuries in Asia, and soy remained inside the Asian region until the modern era.

Matthew Roth's *Magic Bean* (2018) focuses on the American innovators who promoted soy there. Although the United States grew almost no soy at the beginning of the 20th century, soy became the nation's largest agricultural export commodity in a few decades by "one of the most remarkable success stories of twentieth-century American agriculture" (Roth 2018, 1). Rather than American people coming to enjoy Asian tastes, however, they initially focused on the roots, leaves, or stems of the plant (not the bean) as a means to restore soil fertility and for livestock greenfeed. During WWI, however, soy bean as an oilseed suddenly caught the attention of the United States when it found itself importing huge amounts of soy oil from Asia. The following years saw the establishment of the American Soybean Association as well as a US Department of Agriculture expedition to Asia specifically to investigate soy and collect the seeds. New Deal strategies led to reduced production of other crops and increased soy cultivation in the country. Around the same time, soy meal became important to the livestock industry as a protein component of concentrated feed. When the American modern livestock industry model was introduced to the world, the global demand for soy increased along with it.

The expansion of soy to South America was more aggressive. In Brazil, Japanese immigrants had long cultivated some soy, but it was the geopolitical and agro-industrial urgency of the early 1970s that rapidly increased soy cultivation there. When the USSR purchased large amounts of US grain in the so-called "great grain robbery" of 1973 (Morgan 1979), it distorted the grain market and led the United States to place an export embargo on soy. Although the actual embargo lasted only six days (Mitsuishi 2014), it was enough to urge the Japanese government to diversify its soy suppliers, because Japan had become completely dependent on US grain exports by then. The Japanese government made a huge financial investment as official development assistance (ODA), and the Japan International Cooperation Agency (JICA) provided human resources and technological support to promote soy production in South America. Cerrado's acid soil and tropical latitude were far from ideal for growing temperate plant of soy. This hard work of three-decade Japanese-Brazilian PRODECER project is still presented as a JICA's "success" story (Aoki 2002). The Brazilian and Argentinean state-owned agricultural research companies during the 1970s also developed "tropical soy," that is better suited to longer photoperiods and higher temperatures in South American landscapes and subtropical climates (Oliveira and Hecht 2016).

The Western agribusiness soon became the main players in South American soy. The so-called ABCD companies (Archer-Daniels-Midland, Bunge, Cargill, and Louis Dreyfus), the four largest multinational grain traders, used their financial, logistical, organizational, and informational resources and their biotechnology and agrochemical innovations to establish a South American "Soybean Republic" (Turzi 2011; Murphy et al. 2012; Oliveira and Hecht 2016). On the demand side, China changed its soy policy from domestic production to import dependency to adjust their agricultural and industrial structures to be accepted into the World Trade Organization (WTO). China reduced tariffs on soy bean imports in 1996 while it welcomed foreign direct investment (FDI) in the food and livestock industries, which rapidly increased demand for soy in China, soon making it the world's largest importer, taking in more than half of all globally traded soy (Hiraga 2012; Oliveira and Hecht 2016).

Large-scale agro-industrial production of soy is mostly mechanized, chemicalized, and capital-intensive, and soy exports are mostly dominated by big business. Again and again, the rapid expansion of soy production has enriched some while depriving many other people of their livelihood. The power of soy was strengthened with its genetically modified version, as big business expands their rights to intellectual properties and intervenes to local politics (Lapegna 2016; Leguizamón 2020). In Paraguay, soy became the nation's most profitable export commodity in the 2000s, dispossessing many people of farmland and forest and spreading pollution. *La soja mata* (soy kills) became a slogan of protest movements (Hetherington 2020).

In this way, soy has become a global commodity, a topic of trade disputes, a representative of power, a cause of massacres, and thus a crop deeply embedded in local and global political economies.

Soy as a versatile "flex crop"

Another characteristic of soy that calls attention is its versatility. The fact that it has multiple and flexible uses is often regarded positively, and soy is praised for being "versatile and cheap" (Prodöhl 2013), a "magic bean" (Roth 2018), and a "miracle crop" (Khurshid 2017 and others). Rather than being soy's intrinsic nature, this versatility is also a result of active human efforts in the last century or two.

Traditionally, Asian people ate soy foods, typically made from whole beans and often fermented. Today, most soy is crushed first. In 2020/2021, for instance, about 85% of all soy grown in the world was crushed (USDA 2023). The main purpose of crushing soy bean is to produce oil (fat) and meal (protein), which are then used to make hundreds of derivative materials for a variety of industries, including food and non-food manufacturing, animal feed, and fuel. As Prodöhl (2023) put it, soy today is for "fat, feed, and sometimes food."

In contrast to so-called traditional Asian soy foods, the industrialization and commodification of soy tend to be considered Western projects in previous literature. About a century ago, American agrostologist William Morse published a diagram presenting the multiple usages of soy (Figure I.1). He listed like glycerin and explosives, enamels and varnish, and soap stock. However, the diagram also included soy flour for bakeries and soy meal for infant food, edible oils and butter or lard substitutes from soy oil, and various soy food products from dried beans and green beans. As many of these products seem unlikely to have been in common use as foods at the time, the diagram suggests Morse had a strong interest in introducing more soy into the American diet.

A few decades later, Henry Ford, probably the most famous American innovator of soy, experimented with more industrial uses. Ford introduced his "soybean car" in 1941, which served to notify the American people of soy's industrial usage. In fact, despite the name, the exact ingredients of the car's plastic panels are unknown, and it never went into production (The

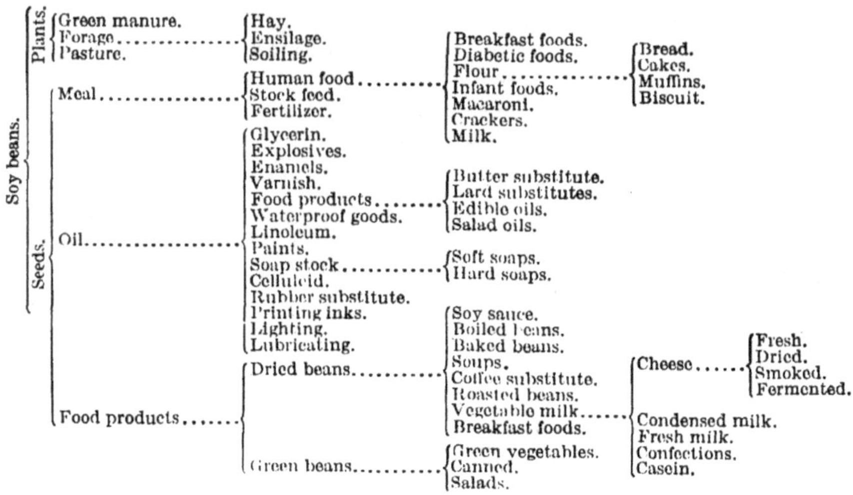

Figure I.1 William Morse's diagram showing the various ways soy was utilized in the United States.

Source: Adapted from Morse (1918, 5).

Henry Ford 2024). For Ford, investigating the multiple uses of soy was "his private hobby" (Roth 2018, 92). In the years after the Great Depression, there was some economic motivation for Ford and other "chemurgy" enthusiasts to promote the industrial use of agricultural products: if farmers could increase the sales of their agricultural crops, they would have more purchasing power as consumers of industrial goods. Soon, however, the experiments of these "chemurgists" were disturbed by the outbreak of WWII (Roth 2018), and they were mostly forgotten in the following age of petrochemistry.

In Europe, Germany took enthusiastically to exploring the many applications of soy, especially in the 1920s to 1930s. German chemists and oil-milling companies developed ways to extract more oil out of soy and to refine the oil to eliminate "offensive" tastes and colors. The Germans used soy oil primarily to produce margarine and soap. Margarine was promoted as a cheaper substitute for butter and animal fat, and soy-based lecithin and casein also substituted for the same elements made from animal resources. Prodöhl (2023) explored these German innovations and argued that the Germans favored Manchurian soy not only for its availability and cheaper price but also due to political motivations, as it allowed them to stay away from other European empires and establish diplomatic ties with Japan (via Japan's puppet-state of "Manchukuo") before WWII.

It is interesting to note that, while innovating industrial usages of soy products, these Western enthusiasts also tried to introduce soy as a healthy food, beyond being an ingredient of margarine or a substitute for other cooking fats. On the menu of Henry Ford's 1934 "soybean dinner," every dish uses soy in various forms, including salted or buttered beans and soy bread or biscuits (The Henry Ford 2024). Various German soy innovators tried introducing soy flour or other soy food not only for commercial reasons to sell their products but also for health reasons (Prodöhl 2023). Other groups of people also have tried to introduce soy foods beyond Asia. For example, William Shurtleff and Akiko Aoyagi began publishing cookbooks focusing on tofu, miso, and tempeh in the 1970s and created an often-referenced English-language database at soyinfocenter.com. However, these early attempts had limited success, and it was only around the 1990s that soy foods became regular items on the shelves of Western supermarkets (Roth 2018; Prodöhl 2013).

Meanwhile, soy *oil* melded into the Western diet, mainly as a fat substitute in manufactured foods, such as margarine. In the United States, cottonseed oil used to be the dominant ingredient of margarine in the early decades of the 20th century, then soy oil took over after WWII. In 1937, cottonseed oil accounted for 53% of oil and fat ingredients for margarine, while soy accounted for 10%. These proportions had reversed by 1960, with cottonseed oil accounting for 10% and soy oil more than 80% (Figure I.2).

Not only in the United States, which was the world supplier of soy post-WWII, but also globally soy oil became the dominant edible oil and remained so until palm oil overtook it around the 2000s. Palm oil and soy oil continue in a tight race since then (Figure I.3). Thus, the world population has been eating significant amounts of soy oil for decades, although mostly without being aware of it, as soy oil is usually hidden in processed foods or used as cooking oil.

At the same time, soy *meal* became an essential resource for livestock industries as the main protein-feed to support the industrial-meat-complex (Weis 2013). Recent increases of soy imports to Asia, especially to China, are not because of rising demand for tofu or miso but to raise more animals for meat. China became the world's largest pork producer by 2010, producing 50 million metric tons of pork, almost half of the global total (IATP 2011). There has been significant political economy of the deregulation and trade liberalization behind this shift (Hiraga 2012; IATP 2011).

Focusing on "soy-industry"

Christine Du Bois (2008, 209) has described the far-reaching impacts of the soy-industry on ecology, socioeconomic power relations, and cultures. Prodöhl (2023), at the end of her book, asks who this "soy-industry" is,

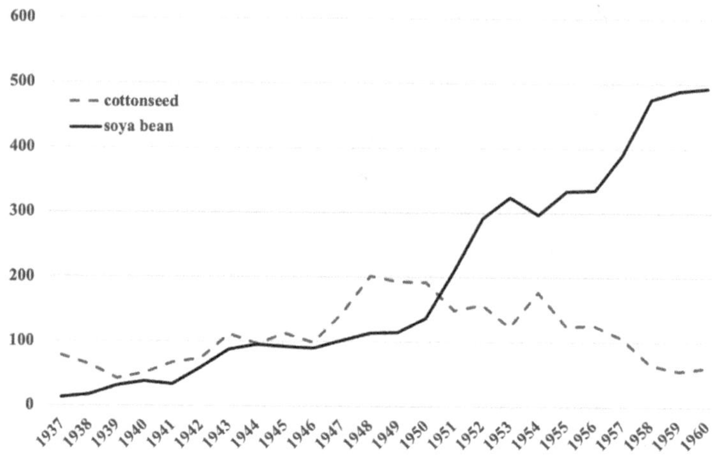

Figure I.2 Volume of cottonseed oil and soy oil used in the production of margarine in the United States, 1937–1960.

Source: Produced by the author based on data from Commonwealth Economic Committee (1950, 1956, and 1962).

pointing out the need to study the composition and formulation of the soy-industry. In my book, the soy-industry is the main focus from the beginning. The "soy-industry" in this book includes soy-crushers, traders of raw materials (soy bean), distributers of soy products (meal and oil), and wide range of manufacturers of oil and protein products in food and non-food industries, as well as the governments, financial institutions, even military and colonial institutions at some stages.

The process of crushing (also called "milling") of soy can mean either extracting oil from the seed to produce oil or removing the oil to produce meal, but the point is that this process always produces both oil *and* meal. The industry's emphasis may shift between the two products according to their prices or market situation at a given time. However, the soy-crushing companies always have to sell *both*. So, the soy-industry constantly strives to develop new products using oil or meal to create demand for both of them and to expand their markets in order to continue their business. Their concern with making profits and surviving in the capitalist world has impacted agriculture and consumers' diets, as well as domestic and global politics and business.

To study the development of the soy-industry and their impacts, I focus more on soy oil. Oil has more versatility to become raw materials for wider range of food and non-food industrial manufacturing and military supply,

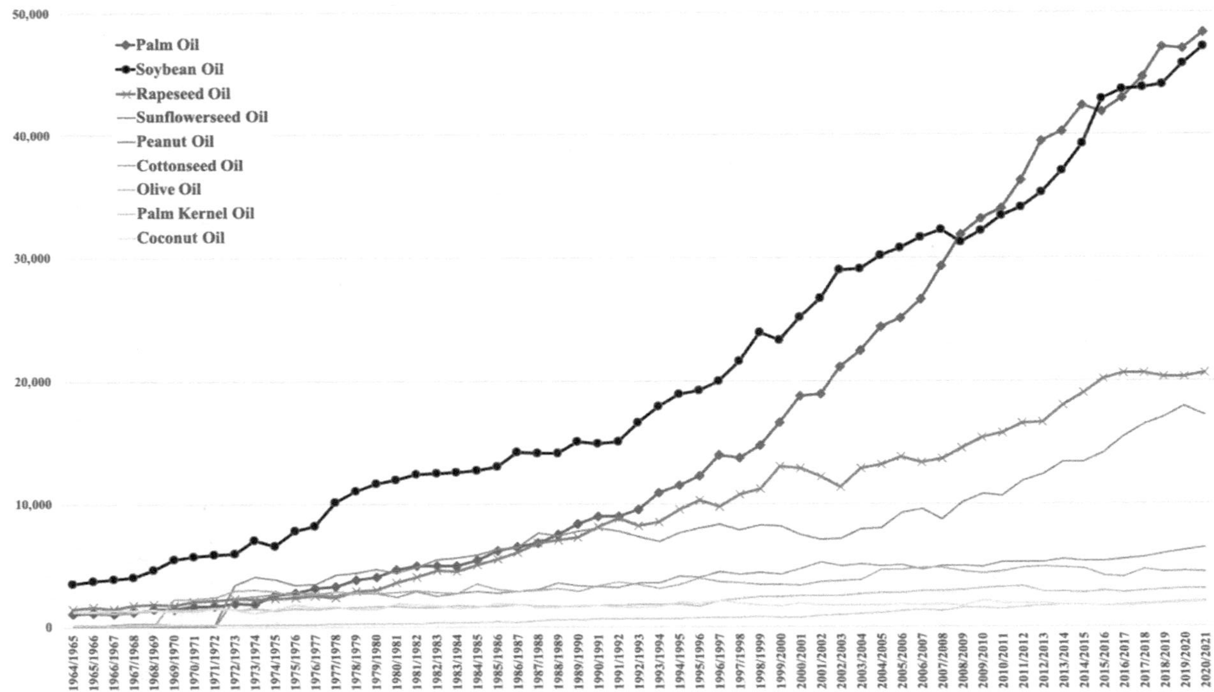

Figure I.3 Volume of vegetable oil consumption for food uses in the world, 1964–2020.

Source: Produced by the author based on the data from USDA FAS Production, Supply and Distribution data.

and oil can be sourced from plant, fish, animal or petrol, and can substitute each other flexibly. Maybe because of such versatility and flexibility beyond food or agriculture, soy oil is less researched in previous literature compared to soy meal used in livestock industries. Still, the history reveals the importance of bio-based oils in the early stage of capitalist world-economy, and vegetable oils have huge impacts on our daily diet today. Therefore, this book focuses on soy oil and the related oils more than soy meal or beans.

Development of versatility for capital accumulation

From the viewpoint of the research on food and capitalism, the versatility of soy, or the interchangeability of organic materials and chemical/mineral materials, contributes to capital accumulation. I find two research trends are relevant to better understand this business history of soy: one focuses on the concepts of appropriationism and substitutionism, which were developed mainly after biotechnologies began modifying seeds in the 1980s; the other centers on the concept of "flex crops," which was developed mainly after the introduction of biofuels, and as more agricultural crops became targets of financial speculation in the 2000s.

Appropriationism and substitutionism

Goodman et al. (1987) proposed appropriationism and substitutionism as a theory of agro-industrial development. They argued that the essential transformation in agriculture, mainly through mechanical innovations, happened between the end of the 19th century and WWI. Capital appropriated agricultural production as more industrialized farm inputs, such as artificial fertilizers, chemical herbicides and pesticides, purchased seeds, and farm machines, replaced farmers' labor and farm-produced organic matter, thus incorporating agriculture into the industrial capital accumulation system (appropriationism). Meanwhile, the development of industrialized, mechanized, large-scale food-processing, like flour-milling, sugar-refining, and oilseed-crushing, transformed rural farm products from food for people into more homogeneous basic raw material inputs for industries—in food-processing or any other non-food manufacturing and chemical industry (substitutionism). The reduction of agricultural products to processed components makes it easier to substitute one crop or nonagricultural raw material for another. These processes of appropriationism and substitutionism allow business to accumulate capital and dominate food systems, impacting both the upstream systems of agriculture and the downstream systems of food.

Flex crops

Technoscientific advances have made soy and other grain and oil crops ever more flexible and multiple in their uses (Borras et al. 2016), with ecological impacts that have drawn critical research attention. For instance, in recent decades, soy oil is increasingly used for biodiesel production (Oliveira and Schneider 2016). The concept of "flex crops" emerged as part of these critical research trends. Flex crops are defined as agricultural products that have "multiple uses (food, feed, fuel, fiber, industrial material, etc.) that can be flexibly interchanged while some consequent supply gaps can be filled by other flex crops" (Borras et al. 2016, 94). Such crops include corn (maize), oil palm, sugarcane, and soy. Among them, soy is considered to be one of the most prominent and established flex crop (Borras et al. 2016). Scholars have focused on how business has utilized the "multiple-ness" and "flexible-ness" of these agricultural crops for corporate strategies to secure profits by hedging risks or taking advantage of changes in market prices and/or in policy frameworks. Describing an extreme stage of the flexible way of accumulating capital from agricultural crops, "the financialization of food and agriculture" discourse argues that these flex crops became financial commodities. Today, the price of soy and other food items is largely determined by financial speculation in future prices and other financial derivatives linked to commodity crops, rather than by trade among farmers or other food-related players (Clapp and Isakson 2018; Hiraga 2018).

While sharing these viewpoints, this book traces back the business history of soy since the dawn of modernization in Asia to study how soy began to be a typical key commodity that is embedded in the capital accumulation structure.

Globalizing and commodifying soy

The existing literature on soy tends to start with its origins in Asia, but then skip quickly to soy in the United States, and, later, in South America and China. Not always but often, they tend to give the impression that a wonderful and "miraculous" Asian traditional food was industrialized and commodified in the West, leading to its current status as a devastating agribusiness crop impacting local peoples and the environment in the modern globalized and neoliberal world.

Ines Prodöhl's work has extended the globalizing and commodifying history of soy from 1900 to the 1950s. In her *Globalizing the Soybean* (2023), Prodöhl connected three continents through soy, beginning with the soy trade in Manchuria, although her main focus stays on Germany's development of the soy-processing industries and the United States' deployment of soy products in the agricultural and livestock industries.

At first glance, this book may seem to be on the same topic, that is, the history of soy's globalization and commodification in the 20th century. Yet, my book complements Prodöhl's work by considering the other side of the coin; I explore how Japanese government and big business transformed Manchurian soy into a versatile global commodity, and how the Japanese side exported soy out from Asia to Germany before WWII, then how they imported American soy into Asia after WWII. Based on Japanese historical studies and sources, I argue that the foundation of soy's globalization and commodification was established before soy disseminated out of Asia beginning in the 19th century.

In this business history of soy, I first question how the soy and oil industries developed as modern big businesses, using the vivid case of modernizing Japan. I demonstrate how these businesses shifted from manufacturing fertilizer and non-food industrial materials to developing military supplies, and then to supplying cheap calories. Second, I investigate the more fundamental question of how capitalist development transformed soy itself, as well as our daily diet.

Why Japan so vividly demonstrates soy's transformation

The business history of soy around Japan and Manchuria since the 19th century is less known, but I argue that this case strikingly demonstrates the process of the development of the soy-industry and how it transformed soy from a traditional Asian food into a dominant global commodity. In doing so, I provide a fundamental understanding of the related political economy.

The reason I focus on the Japanese case has little to do with the traditional uses of soy food in Japan—far from it. The modern soy-industry began mass-producing soy oil when there was no market for it in the country. Japan's Food balance sheet data show that average fat-nutrient (lipid) supply to a Japanese person from soy oil was zero in 1911–1915. The average supply of fat-nutrient from all oil and fat items increased by about 30 times in the following century, from 1.3 grams daily per capita in the 1911–1915 period to 36.9 grams in 2010, during which the Japanese soy and oil companies poured enormous efforts into expanding their markets.

The Japanese soy-industry did not develop from the small-scale, rural cottage industry of processing domestic soy for food. Rather, it began with large-scale capital-intensive mechanical factories, built to crush overseas soy cultivated in Manchuria. The Japanese government and big business have deeply involved in this progress from the very beginning, as I explore in this book. Once the capital-intensive mode of mass-production was established, the soy businesses needed to continue selling their products. Over the years, Japanese companies have taken energetic, and sometimes drastic, actions to increase demand for oil and meal, transforming soy and impacting our daily diet.

Because of this drastic increase of soy oil supply from zero in a century, and of the involvement of big players who mainly used the imported soy from the beginning, I believe this business history of soy with modernizing Japan can provide a vivid case that can shed a new light and improve our understanding of soy's globalizing and commodified progress.

Theoretical frameworks

To study the business history of soy, this book employs the following approaches: (1) it considers how mass-production and mass-distribution systems expanded soy's versatility and product markets; (2) it delves into how business and government used soy in imperial, military, and economic development strategies; and ultimately (3) it positions soy as a critical element in the development of the capitalist world-economy. Based on these theoretical frameworks, I argue that it was big business and governments that transformed soy into a versatile global commodity, much more than people's demand or any natural characteristic of soy per se.

The impact of mass-production and mass-distribution on soy

The classic works of Alfred D. Chandler (1977 and others) explain how modern big business since the 19th century has made significant changes in production and supply systems for many products. Innovations in transportation and communication technologies, especially railroads, steamships, telegraphs, and cables, enabled mass-production and mass-distribution in many industries for the first time. Simultaneously, many businesses turned to professional managers who worked to develop new products and expand into new markets. They introduced new technologies and coordinated continuous large-volume production, which requires continuous mass-distribution, thus mass-sales, to secure continuous profit.

Along with the machinery and automobile industries, modern big business took over a significant part of food-processing industries, including soy and oils. They built capital-intensive, large-scale, mechanized food-processing factories and began supplying large volumes of standardized foodstuffs, with the company name on the packages. Chandler studied how the managers of flour mills introduced the continuous-processing system with newly developed machinery and technologies of steel rollers, gradual reduction, multiple grinding, and other related inventions. The professional managers coordinated the mass-production of high-quality flour at a low unit cost (Chandler 1977, 251).

The mechanical mass-processing of wheat flour impacted not only business practices but also the characteristics of wheat and its role in agriculture and food systems. To mass-produce flour, the mechanical factories required large volumes of wheat as a raw material. Thus, the introduction of roller-milling to the United States around the 1870s encouraged the large-scale cultivation of harder spring-wheat in North America. The mass-production of flour enabled the mass-production of bread and other flour-based processed food, which in turn led to the development of modern bakery and food-processing industries. That was the beginning of what Anthony Winson (2013) called the "Industrial Diet."

Mass-production systems also impacted the characteristics of the flour they supplied. Traditionally, wheat was stone-milled locally, with the mills sometimes powered by water or wind. Such stone-milled flour was coarser and maintained more nutritional value, although it was more perishable because of the oils in the wheatgerm. Hence, flour was mainly consumed locally. However, when steam-powered steel-roller milling machinery was introduced, the new process produced finer, whiter, "patent" flour, which gained better storage quality by losing the nutritious but spoilable elements. This new characteristic of machine-milled flour enabled long-distance trade, both domestic and international, and encouraged consolidation in the milling industry and the related food-processing industries (Goodman, Sorj, and Wilkinson 1987, 61; Winson 2013, 22).

This book finds similar impacts on soy and explores how mass-production and mass-distribution transformed soy from a local food into a raw material for various industries, and thus making it a global commodity. The Japanese government and their collaborating *zaibatsu* supported Japanese big business and the colonial institution of the South Manchuria Railway as they established the modern soy-industry in Manchuria. I argue that, because their mass-production and mass-distribution systems require continuous mass-sales, the soy-industry has constantly worked, sometimes desperately, to develop new soy products and expand soy markets from fertilizer to non-food industrial and military applications and then to processed food products.

The role of soy in the "visible hands" of big business and big government

Small-scale bakeries and tofu-makers still exist in Japanese towns today, and they offer an imaginary origin story for food-processing industries; people tend to imagine that food companies began as small businesses based on local agricultural cultivation, then grew bigger in later years. The history indicates, however, that many of today's big food businesses started out big, and that they have impacted our food systems significantly.

Adam Smith's famous "invisible hand" of the market was replaced by the "visible hand" of professional managers by the late 19th century, and they became the most powerful institution in the United States' economy (Chandler 1977). Large companies dominated the new capital-intensive scale-dependent technology of mass-production in various industries, and the dynamics of big business significantly impacted the "wealth of nations" in the century from the 1880s to the 1980s (Chandler et al. 1997). The "visible hand" of government has also been active in the development of modern economies, at least since the time of the Industrial Revolution. Lars Magnusson (2009) argued that "real-world economies are characterized by a combination of the invisible hand of market mechanisms and the visible hand of public intervention" (15). "Big business" and "big government" together contribute to economic growth, as "the large corporation lives in a world partially defined and regulated by government institutions" (McCraw 1997, 526).

In addition, government intervention tended to be stronger for latecomers to industrial development. Compared with the governments of the United Kingdom and the United States, which led industrial development in the world-economy, the governments of France, Italy, and Spain played more active and significant roles in introducing newer, more capital-intensive industries in their countries (Chandler et al. 1997, ch.1). Japan was a much latercomer than these European countries, and it is common knowledge that the Japanese government has strongly supported the industrial development of the nation; Japanese history textbooks teach students some modernization policies, like the "promotion of industries" (殖産興業), the policy that the Meiji government itself built steel and machinery industries and then transferred them to private companies, or of "increasing wealth and military power" (富国強兵), the policy of accumulating capital for Japan's industrial and military development to stand against the Western superpowers. After Japan was defeated in WWII and began rapid economic growth within a decade, the Japanese government facilitated a powerfully protectionist and developmental environment for industries. Some aspects are known as the "convoy system" (護送船団方式), wherein the government and bureaucracy protected financial and other important industries, or as *gyosei-shido* (行政指導), meaning the government or administrative offices giving official or unofficial guidance to business. McCraw (1997) argued that Japan has a "national economic bureaucracy," which includes the Ministry of Finance, the central bank (Bank of Japan), and the Ministry of International Trade and Industry (MITI).

Along the way, the Japanese government has consistently collaborated with big capital groups. The latter have been known by different names in different eras, from *zaibatsu* and *Konzern* (from German, meaning "concerns") in the prewar era, to corporate groups or *keiretsu* in the post-WWII era. MORIKAWA Hidemasa defined *zaibatsu* as a "diversified enterprise group exclusively owned and controlled by a single wealthy family" (Morikawa 1997, 307), though their various backgrounds formed a variety of groups, and their boundaries are vague. Diversity is an important characteristic of Japanese *zaibatsu* and their trading sectors, or *sogo-shosha*, which translates as "general trading company." The diversity of their business interests is sometimes described as "from cup noodle to missile." While these corporations' involvement in energy or heavy industries tends to draw attention, they also have been deeply involved in the agriculture and food systems of Japan. They were significant contributors to the establishment of the modern food industry, including soy, oil, flour, sugar, and other basic ingredients and food-processing industries, as well as livestock, supermarket, and fast-food industries, as the following chapters demonstrate. Although *zaibatsu* were officially dissolved after WWII, their impacts still exist in Japanese society, and their *sogo-shosha* are still active and dominant not only in Japan but also globally (Hall 2020).

Based on this context, this book focuses on how the "visible hands" of Japanese big business and big government have used soy in their strategies for imperial, military, and economic development. I argue that their main purpose had little to secure food for the Japanese people, but rather to accumulate capital to support the Japanese industrial revolution, to supplement the lack of petroleum resources to wage wars, and to expand their economic and political power in Asia and in the world-economy.

Soy and oil as critical elements in the development of the capitalist world-economy

Japan's state-building project did not happen in isolation. On the contrary, modern Japan and the soy-industry were established in interaction with the development of the capitalist world-economy. This book explores the historical development of the political economy around soy by positioning it in Japan's development in the capitalist world-economy. To do so, I loosely base my analysis on the world system theory via the Food Regime frameworks developed by agri-food political economists. The Food Regime is a historical concept, and Food Regime analysis studies capitalist development without separating agriculture and industry, nor limiting its scope to within national boundaries. Instead, it situates agriculture and food as one of the central components deeply embedded in the structure of capital accumulation in the world-economy.

The Food Regime frameworks were developed based on Immanuel Wallerstein's concept of the world system and Michel Aglietta's concept of the *regulation* of capital accumulation (McMichael 2013). Harriet Friedmann and Philip McMichael first explored the role of agriculture in the development of the capitalist world-economy in their landmark 1989 article, "Agriculture and the State System: The Rise and Decline of National Agriculture, 1870 to the Present" (Friedmann and McMichael 1989). They originally framed two regimes: the First Food Regime from 1870 to 1914, under British hegemony, and the Second Food Regime from 1947 to 1973, under US hegemony. In the former, European countries shifted to industrial economies while importing wheat and meat from the settler states and tropical raw materials from their colonies; wheat was a main commodity exported from North America to Europe to cheaply feed factory workers. In the latter, which starts after the nation-state system was established, the transnational restructuring of agricultural sectors was motivated by the overproduction of US grain and oilseeds.

The original Food Regime analysis was based on historical cases around the Atlantic. The international division of labor was built across the Atlantic, in which North American family-farmers supplied cheap food to the urban factory workers in Western Europe: wheat was transformed from food for people into a raw material for food-processing industries and into a global commodity in the world-economy, as agriculture became a component of industrial capital accumulation (Friedmann 1991). Then, the United States became a major exporter of wheat and soy to the rest of the world, first in the form of food aid and then through commercial marketing. The United States supplied their grain and oilseeds strategically to the world to support the development of the meat (soy-corn-animals) complex and the durable (processed) food complex by exporting US models and integrating the receiving countries into the US Food Regime (Friedmann and McMichael 1989). Food and agriculture has been deeply embedded in the system of capital accumulation, and we now have a capitalist food system (Holt-Giménez 2017).

It is interesting to note that the Food Regime frameworks developed by agri-food scholars more or less overlap with the global economy frameworks discussed in the business history literature. Geoffrey G. Jones (2005) framed the first global economy from the 1880s to 1929 and the beginning of a new global economy from 1950 to 1979. They may well coincide because the modern big business demanded large volumes of raw materials and foodstuffs for their machinery and workers, at the same time demanding market expansion to sell their manufactured products. It was also the time that multinational traders became active, such as grain traders. Jones (1998, 2005) argued that people, capital, and goods moved across national borders and multinational trade developed in the first globalized economy of the 19th century. The numbers of multinational businesses, and their scale, grew more rapidly from the 1880s onward, with increased trade of natural resources and agricultural crops from the "new world," to be used as raw materials and food supplies that supported the industrial development in their host countries. Many of the Western multinational grain traders began their business around this era: Archer-Daniels-Midland originated in 1902, Bunge in 1818, Cargill in 1865, and Louis Dreyfus in 1851. These traders actively exported grain from North and South America to Europe in the free-trade regime that prevailed until the crisis of 1929 (Morgan 1979). They have adjusted their business and organizations, but still these "ABCD companies" are dominant today, said to control about 90% of the global grain trade, including wheat, corn (maize), sugar, oilseeds like soy bean and cottonseed, and vegetable oils like palm oil (Murphy et al. 2012).

These global progress has impacted Japan, of course. Many of Japanese *sogo-shosha* traders were also established in the early stages of modern Japan's development as it entered the capitalist world-economy. Soy from Manchuria and some other agricultural crops played significant roles as key commodities for them to process and to trade as a means to accumulate capital and to increase Japan's political, economic, imperial, and military power in the Asian region. The *sogo-shosha* like Mitsui and Mitsubishi, Suzuki Shoten, and Itochu, Marubeni were the main players as the "government's traders" of *zaibatsu*, a part of *Konzern*, or as the "general trading companies" by changing their names and forms in the historical periods. Many of these *sogo-shosha* are still active in today's Japan and the world (Hall 2020).

With these main actors—the Japanese government, Japanese big business, including the *zaibatsu* and their trading companies, and Japanese colonial institutions and military at some stages—Japan has behaved like a "core" country in the Asian context, although deciding whether Japan is a "core" or "semi-peripheral" country in world-system theory is a question beyond the scope of this book. Japan was, at least, an imperial power that procured resources, labor forces, and markets from its empire, including Manchuria, China, Korea, Taiwan, and parts of Southeast Asia and the Pacific islands, to develop the Japanese economy.

By integrating business history and the political economy of agriculture and food, I aim to illuminate the roles of soy and oil in the development of the capitalist world-economy.

Outline of the book

This book's study is based on Japanese historical documents that are less known by English-language academia. The main materials include corporate histories and business reports for major oil, soap, and food companies, as well as of traders including Mitsui, Mitsubishi, Marubeni, and Itochu. The basic information of the main companies and their current situation are summarized in the Appendix. The book also draws on the accumulated Japanese literature that delves into *zaibatsu* and *sogo-shosha* and their roles in the capitalist development of Japan. Reports from the South Manchuria Railway and classified war-era documents from the ex-imperial university library of Kyoto University were also studied. Although they may not be the primary historical materials, I hope to build a macro-structural understanding for a longer period first.

The book is loosely structured in chronological order, while focusing on specific characteristics in each stage: Chapter 1 briefly outlines the pre-history of soy and vegetable oils in Japan as the background. Chapter 2 begins the business history of soy along with Japan's modernization by exploring the development of the Manchurian soy-industry and the export of soy products (bean, meal, and oil) as a part of Japan's state-building project from the 19th century to WWI. Chapter 3 focuses on corporate efforts to expand soy's versatility in multiple markets for business survival and as a colonial strategy in the interwar period. Chapter 4 delves into the drastic change before and after Japan's defeat in 1945, as Japanese companies shifted their sourcing of resources from Asian oil crops to US soy, and their markets from military supplies to food products. Then, Chapter 5 explores the efforts from supply side, describing how big government and big business actively increased the demand for oil and meal in post-WWII Japan. The conclusion chapter provides an overview of the shifts in soy products and markets, business and government strategies, and the role of soy and oil in food systems and capitalist history across the four stages explored from Chapter 2 to Chapter 5. The conclusion chapter also includes a table that provides an overall snapshot of the book's entire structure and discussion points.

This book focuses on the original transformation and globalization of soy up to the 1970s, when mass-produced soy oil and meal had been established as basic foodstuff. The author well acknowledges soy's dramatic transformation and its related global political economy and geopolitics in the following age of globalization and the climate crisis, the phase that some scholars framed as the "Third Food Regime" or "Corporate Food Regime" (McMichael 2013 among others). There has been rather accumulated research on these issues, some of which I mentioned earlier in this introduction chapter. In addition to that, the formation of the "Third Food Regime" and its characteristics have been controversial compared to more established First and Second Food Regimes, the topic still discussed with unsettled agreement among the agri-food scholars. Similarly, the ecological sustainability questions around soy are significantly important recent issues that many scholars are now conducting surveys and research. These issues on soy are important, but they require separate full-scale research for another book or more. Meanwhile, this book keeps its focus on the original transformation of soy since the 19th century, which is little known to the world. I hope this understanding of the very beginning of soy's transformation and its political economy can deepen the discussion on the further transformation and globalization of soy in later decades and its relationship with the ecological sustainability questions.

This book focuses on Japan, yet the story has global implications. Vegetable oils, including soy oil, are made cheaply and thus can be found almost everywhere in our food systems today. Soy meal is a key feed that supports industrial livestock production, which supplies cheap meat and dairy products. Global demand for soy is said to increase more as emerging economies develop. Questions remain regarding whether soy offers hope for a sustainable diet and whether its contributions to the climate crisis can be mitigated. I hope this book can shed a new light on these global discussions.

Note

1 "Manchuria" is a historical term that refers to a vaguely delineated region of Northeast China. The term was mainly used by foreigners, including the Japanese, and it must be differentiated from "Manchukuo," the name of the puppet-state built by the Japanese in 1932–1945. Manchuria is not an official name used in China. Nevertheless, it is used in this book as it is the term most widely known outside of China for the general region under discussion.

Bibliography

In English

Borras Jr, S. M., Franco, J. C., Isakson, S. R., Levidow, L., and Vervest, P. (2016) "The Rise of Flex Crops and Commodities: Implications for Research", *The Journal of Peasant Studies*, 43(1), pp. 93–115.

Britannica (2024) "Soybean," The Encyclopedia Britannica, available at: www.britannica.com/plant/soybean (accessed January 1, 2024).

Chandler, A. (1977) *The Visible Hand: The Managerial Revolution in American Business*, The Belknap Press of Harvard University Press.

Chandler, A., Amatori, F., and Hikino, T. eds. (1997) *Big Business and the Wealth of Nations*, Cambridge University Press.

Clapp, J. and Isakson, S. R. (2018). *Speculative Harvests: Financialization*, Food, and Agriculture, Agrarian Change & Peasant Studies, Fernwood Publishing.

Commonwealth Economic Committee (1950, 1956, and 1962) *Vegetable Oils and Oilseeds: A Summary of Figures of Production, Trade and Consumption Relating to Groundnuts, Cottonseed, Linseed, Soya Beans, Coconut and Oil Palm Products, Olive Oil, and Other Oilseeds and Oils*, UK Stationery Office.

Du Bois, C. M. (2018). *The Story of Soy*, Reaktion Books.

Du Bois, C. M., Tan, C. B., and Mintz, S. eds. (2008) *The World of Soy*, University of Illinois Press.

Friedmann, H. (1991) "Changes in the International Division of Labor: Agri-food Complexes and Export Agriculture", in Friedland, W. H., Busch, L., Buttel, F. H., and Rudy, A. P. (eds.), *Towards a New Political Economy of Agriculture* (pp. 65–93), Westview Press.

Friedmann, H. and McMichael, P. (1989) "Agriculture and the State System: The Rise and Decline of National Agricultures, 1870 to the Present", *Sociologia Ruralis*, 29(2), pp. 93–117.

Goodman, D., Sorj, B., and Wilkinson, J. (1987) *From Farming to Biotechnology*, Basil Blackwell.
Hall, D. (2020). "National Food Security through Corporate Globalization: Japanese Strategies in the Global Grain Trade since the 2007–2008 Food Crisis", *The Journal of Peasant Studies*, 47(5), pp. 993–1029.
Hetherington, K. (2020) *The Government of Beans: Regulating Life in the Age of Monocrops*, Duke University Press.
Hiraga, M. (2012) "How Does Trade Liberalisation Facilitate Nutrition Transition? Examples of Structural Changes in China and India's Vegetable Oil and Animal Feed Supply Chains and their Dietary Impact", MSc thesis submitted to the Centre for Food Policy, Department of Sociology, School of Arts and Social Sciences, City University London.
Hiraga, M. (2018). "Financialization in Japanese Agri-Food Regimes: Uncovering the Role of *sogo-shosha* in Global Soy Investment", in Bjorkhaug, H., Magnan, A., and Lawrence, G. (eds.), *The Financialization of Agri-Food Systems: Contested Transformations* (pp. 156–175), Routledge.
Holt-Giménez, E. (2017) *A Foodie's Guide to Capitalism: Understanding the Political Economy of What We Eat*, Monthly Review Press.
IATP (Institute for Agriculture and Trade Policy) (2011) "Feeding China's Pigs: Implications for the Environment, China's Smallholder Farmers and Food Security", available at www.iatp.org/files/2011_04_25_FeedingChinasPigs_0.pdf (accessed April 7, 2012).
Jones, G. (1998) "Multinational Trading Companies in History and Theory", in Jones, G. (ed.), *The Multinational Traders* (pp. 1–21), Routledge International Studies in Business History, Routledge.
Jones, G. (2005) *Multinationals and Global Capitalism: From the Nineteenth to the Twenty-first Century*, Oxford University Press.
Khurshid, H., Baig, D., Jan, S. A., Arshad, M., and Khan, M. A. (2017). "Miracle Crop: The Present and Future of Soybean Production in Pakistan", *MOJ Biol Med*, 2(1), pp. 189–191.
Lapegna, P. (2016) *Soybeans and Power: Genetically Modified Crops, Environmental Politics, and Social Movements in Argentina*, Oxford University Press.
Leguizamón, A. (2020). *Seeds of Power: Environmental Injustice and Genetically Modified Soybeans in Argentina*, Duke University Press.
Magnusson, L. (2009) Nation, State and the Industrial Revolution: The Visible Hand, Routledge Explorations in Economic History 45, Routledge.
McCraw, T. K. (1997) 'Government, Big Business, and the Wealth of Nations', in A. D. Chandler, F. Amatori, and T. Hikino (eds.), *Big Business and the Wealth of Nations* (pp. 522–545), Cambridge University Press.
McMichael, P. (2013) *Food Regimes and Agrarian Questions*, Fernwood Publishing.
Morgan, D. (1979) *Merchants of Grain: The Power and Profits of the Five Giant Companies at the Center of the World's Food Supply*, Viking-Penguin.
Morikawa, H. (1997) 'Japan: Increasing Organizational Capabilities of Large Industrial Enterprises, 1880s–1980s', in A.D. Chandler, F. Amatori, and T. Hikino (eds.), *Big Business and the Wealth of Nations* (pp. 305–335), Cambridge University Press.

Morse, W. (1918) *The Soy Bean: Its Culture and Uses, USDA Farmers' Bulletin 973*, available at https://digital.library.unt.edu/ark:/67531/metadc96561/ (accessed January 4, 2024).
Murphy, S., Burch, D., and Clapp, J. (2012) "Cereal Secrets. The World's Largest Grain Traders and Global Agriculture', *Oxfam Research Reports*. Oxfam International. Available at www.oxfam.org/en/research/cereal-secrets-worlds-largest-grain-traders-and-global-agriculture (accessed August 5, 2012)
Oliveira, G. and Hecht, S. (2016). "Sacred Groves, Sacrifice Zones and Soy Production: Globalization, Intensification and Neo-nature in South America", in Oliveira, G. and Hecht, S. (eds). *Soy, Globalization, and Environmental Politics in South America* (pp. 1–35), Routledge.
Oliveira, G. and Schneider, M. (2016) "The Politics of Flexing Soybeans: China, Brazil and Global Agroindustrial Restructuring", *Journal of Peasant Studies*, 43(1), pp. 167–194.
Prodöhl, I. (2013) "Versatile and Cheap: A Global History of Soy in the First Half of the Twentieth Century", *Journal of Historical Geography*, 8(3), pp. 461–482.
Prodöhl, I. (2023). *Globalizing the Soybean: Fat, Feed, and Sometimes Food, c.1900–1950*, Routledge.
Roth, M. (2018) *Magic Bean: The Rise of Soy in America*, University Press of Kansas.
The Henry Ford (2024) Popular Research Topics "Soybean Car", available at www.thehenryford.org/collections-and-research/digital-resources/popular-topics/soy-bean-car (accessed January 28, 2024).
Turzi, M. (2011) "The Soybean Republic", *Yale Journal of International Affairs*, 6, pp. 59–68.
Weis, T. (2013) "The Meat of the Global Food Crisis", *The Journal of Peasant Studies*, 40(1), pp. 65–85.
Winson, A. (2013) *The Industrial Diet: The Degradation of Food and the Struggle for Healthy Eating*, New York University Press.

In Japanese (with English translation by the author)

Aoki, H. (2002) *The Struggle History of Soy in Brazil* (青木公 [2002]『ブラジル大豆攻防史：国際協力20年の結実』国際協力出版会).
Mitsuishi, S. (2014) "The US Grain Export Embargo", (三石誠司 [2014]「アメリカの穀物輸出制限」『フードシステム研究』第20巻第4号、pp. 372–385).

Websites

FAOstat www.fao.org/faostat/en/#home, Food and Agriculture Organization of the United Nations.
MAFF *Food Balance Sheet* (農林水産省「食料需給表」) www.maff.go.jp/j/zyukyu/fbs/, Ministry of Agriculture, Forestry and Fisheries (Japan).
SoyInfo Center www.soyinfocenter.com, SOYINFO CENTER (Willam Shurtleff and Akiko Aoyagi).
USDA PDS data https://apps.fas.usda.gov/psdonline/app/index.html#/app/home, United States Department of Agriculture Foreign Agricultural Service (USA).

1 Premodern history of soy and vegetable oils in Japan

Introduction

Before we delve into the birth of the soy-industry and Japan's modernization, this chapter outlines the history of soy and vegetable oils in Japan until the end of the feudal Edo period (1603–1867). For centuries, Japanese people ate soy foods made from the whole beans, often fermented, but they did not extract oil from soy. They did press oil from other plants, including perilla or sesame, and later from rapeseed or cottonseed, but this was mainly for rituals and illumination rather than for food. The Imperial Court, and then the feudal governments, took special care of the production and distribution of vegetable oils by protecting authorized craftsmen and trading organizations. As the large cities of Osaka and Edo (today's Tokyo) developed in feudal era, vegetable oils served as precious and major fuel for lighting, thus becoming a very important commodity for the government to secure law and order in business centers and urban areas. The premodern history demonstrates that, even when they were manually produced on a small scale with simple tools, vegetable oils were already a very political commodity.

Vegetable oils for rituals and illumination

Tempura is a well-known Japanese "traditional" food. Its origin is unclear and disputable, although it is most often said to have appeared in the early modern age in the capital city of Edo as a street food fried in sesame oil. Also around that time, some oils were used to cook vegetarian food (*shojin-ryori*) in Buddhist temples (Hirano and Kobayashi 1976). In short, there were a few fried foods in Japan, but they were never part of the ordinary diet (although ghosts and monster cats were known to lick oil from lamps in Japanese folklore). For centuries, the vegetable oils that were produced in Japan were important, not as food for human consumption but as lighting oil.

DOI: 10.4324/9781032678733-2

Golden Flower is an often-quoted historical book on vegetable oil development in Japan. It was first published in 1902 by OOURA Mankichi, the president of a vegetable-oil-trading company. It was revised in 1944, and a re-revised and enlarged edition was published in 1948, adding HIRANO Shigeyuki as an editor. Ooura said he wrote the book, based on his decades of experience in the industry, and historical materials he had gathered, because there was no other comprehensive history on the development of Japan's vegetable oil industry (Ooura and Hirano eds. 1948, 13). According to *Golden Flower*, Japanese people had produced vegetable oils for centuries by pressing oilseeds like *egoma* (perilla), sesame, or *hashibami* (a kind of hazelnut). They began pressing rapeseed and cottonseed in the Middle Ages. Vegetable oils were important to the authorities, especially after Buddhism was introduced to Japan in the 6th century, and the authorities began to use the religion to govern the country. Vegetable oils were produced by specially authorized craftsmen, with the product dedicated largely to shrines and temples to light their religious rituals, as well as the precious premises. Later, vegetable oils were used to illuminate the houses of the nobility and rich residents in urban areas (Ooura and Hirano eds. 1948, 18). In this way, the authorized craftsmen produced vegetable oils under the protection of the Japanese authorities—the Imperial Court first and then the feudal governments—for hundreds of years.

A famous traditional vegetable oil production site is Ooyamazaki, which is located between Kyoto and Osaka. The shrine of *Rikyu-Hachimangu* in Ooyamazaki is praised as the origin of oil-pressing in Japan (Rikyu-Hachiman n.d.). According to legend, it was here that an oil-pressing tool called the *nagaki* (長木, also known as a *chougi*) was invented around the 850s. Ooyamazaki's craftsmen were granted the exclusive right to use this type of oil press, and they dedicated their oil to shrines and temples. *Nagaki* literally means a long piece of wood, and the press uses the principle of leverage to create pressure to squeeze oil out of perilla seeds. Over two centuries since the Jogan era (859–877), the oil craftsmen of Ooyamazaki were Japan's major suppliers of oil for rituals and illumination.

Another early oil production site is Oriono, part of today's Osaka. There are several legends about the origin of Oriono's oil production, but the most likely story is that a new type of oil press, called a *shimegi*, became popular there around the 1600s. The name literally means "squeezing wood." Oilseeds were pressed by using manual force, as workers knocked wedges between vertical and horizontal pieces of wood from both sides, forcing them apart to increase pressure and squeezing the oil from the seeds at the bottom (see Figure 1.1). Oil craftsmen in Oriono used rapeseed in the *shimegi*, which encouraged increased rapeseed cultivation around Osaka.

In premodern Japan, vegetable oil production was centered in the Western regions, especially around Kyoto, Nara, and Osaka, the traditional

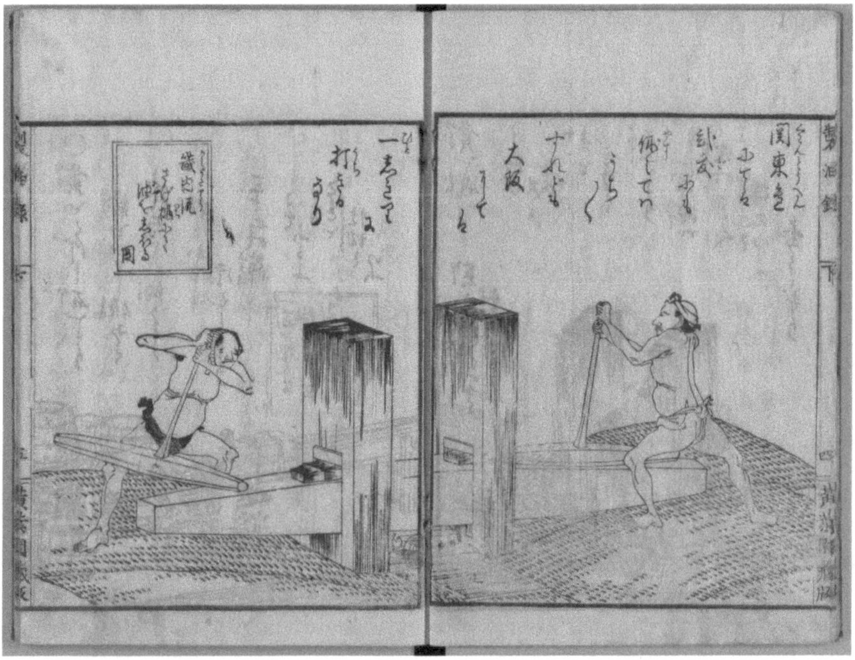

Figure 1.1 Pressing oil with a *shimegi*, with men knocking in wedges from both sides; from OKURA Nagatsune (1836) *Oil Making Record.*

Source: National Diet Library Digital Collections (大蔵永常『製油録 2巻』, [1836]. https://dl.ndl.go.jp/pid/2575821).

capital cities and business centers. According to *Golden Flower*, the Imperial Court and the many shrines and temples located in the area were the major buyers of lighting oil; the local government officials were thus motivated to provide special rights and protections for oil-pressing craftsmen in the area. The climate of Western Japan was suitable for cultivating rapeseed and cottonseed as well (Ooura and Hirano eds. 1948, 71–72).

When the capital city moved to Edo in Eastern Japan in 1603, a new trading route developed from the vegetable oil production sites of Western Japan to the new capital. As Edo grew, vegetable oils became critical for illuminating the city and keeping public order. In this feudal period, when Japanese society developed a self-sustaining domestic economy under a national isolation policy that lasted more than two centuries, vegetable oil became the most consumed commodity following rice, which set the standard for general prices of commodities. It was the most-used illuminating fuel and an essential good for urban life, and the price change of vegetable oil significantly impacted the family budgets of *samurai* and city residents (Ooura and Hirano eds. 1948, 105). In order to maintain the public order of the capital city and the strong political status against the Western Japan, the Edo government actively controlled the vegetable oil supply. It intervened in the production of oilseed and the pressing of vegetable oils, the pricing of vegetable oils, and even in the measuring system and trading system for vegetable oils. In other words, vegetable oils were already political commodities in the premodern era because they were Japan's main lighting fuel.

To summarize, vegetable oils in premodern Japan were largely fuel for illumination. Although food uses of oil were not entirely absent in premodern Japan, they were largely limited to special cuisines for monks or in the capital city of Edo. Because vegetable oils were used to conduct rituals and to illuminate shrines and temples, when religion was used to govern the people, the Imperial Court and the governments in various dynasties protected vegetable oil producers, giving exclusive production rights to specific craftsmen. These factors made vegetable oil a very political commodity even in the premodern era. Later, in the feudal Edo period, vegetable oil was an important commodity because it was crucial for illuminating and keeping public order in the cities, and therefore the government actively promoted oilseed production and protected oil producers. This feudal government's policies "laid the foundation for the vegetable oil industry to develop and flourish in the following modern era," as the authors of *Golden Flower* wrote. Thus, Japan already had developed rather strong government-supported oilseed production and commodity systems before the country began to modernize in the 19th century (Ooura and Hirano eds. 1948, 105).

After Japan's isolation ended and its markets opened to the world in the latter half of 19th century, the traditional oil production sites began to use machine-powered oil presses imported from Europe or the United States. One of the forerunners of the modern oil industry, the oil production company Yokkaichi-seiyu (四日市製油) in Mie prefecture, imported a steam-driven oil-pressing machine in 1882. Another producer, Settsu-seiyu (攝津製油) in Osaka, imported a machine press from the United Kingdom in 1890. In this way, new machine-based oil production techniques were introduced to press traditional oilseeds like rapeseed and cottonseed. However, vegetable oil production developed into a full-scale mechanical-industry, not by processing domestic oilseeds but by processing imported soy bean from Manchuria. As the authors of *Golden Flower* later reflected, "the imported Manchurian soy bean provided the revolutionary trigger for the birth of the vegetable oil industry in Japan" (Ooura and Hirano eds. 1948, 157).

The beginning of soy-crushing and the use of soy meal in China

Meanwhile, soy beans continued to be eaten in Japan, mostly in fermented forms like miso and soy sauce, which are made with the whole bean. In the old days, Japanese people called the soy bean *aze-mame* (levee bean) because they planted it at the edge (*aze*, or levee) of paddy fields (some organic farmers maintain this practice today; see Figure 1.2). The rice grown in the paddy fields and the soy on the surrounding levees were good companions, not only agriculturally but nutritionally, as rice provides carbohydrates and soy provides protein. In this way, Japanese people regarded soy as food, and not as an oilseed, before modernization.

Figure 1.2 Soy planted along the *aze* (levee) next to organic rice paddy fields in Iwaishima, Japan, in 2015. (Photograph by the author.)

Soy is said to originate in China, and there too (including in Manchuria), soy was long regarded as a food rather than a source of oil, while vegetable oils were pressed from other oilseeds like rapeseed and sesame. For example, even in the 1920s, when the American agricultural economist John Lossing Buck researched rural China, he categorized soy beans as legumes, while he categorized rapeseed, sesame, and peanuts as oilseeds (Buck 1930).

It is said that soy-crushing proceeded in China before Japan, although pinpointing the exact beginning would require separate research in Chinese historical records. Various documents available in Japanese from the early 20th century claim that some Chinese people had begun pressing soy at different times, up to a few centuries earlier. In 1924, a report of the South Manchuria Railway wrote that Chinese people had begun pressing soy about three centuries earlier, toward the end of the Ming dynasty (1368–1644); before that, they had used soy in bean form while obtaining their oil from other, higher oil-content seeds like rapeseed or sesame (SMR 1924a, 305). Another report published in the same year said soy-crushing and oil-extraction had begun in Manchuria about a century before (SMR 1924b, 2). A Japanese scholar wrote, in 1942, that the history of the soy-crushing and oil-extracting industry in Manchuria had begun about 80 years earlier (Masuno 1942, 160). Nisshin Oil's president wrote that soy-crushing and oil-extraction began in Manchuria in the middle of the 19th century (Sakaguchi 1987, 58).

The development of Manchuria as a soy supplier

Manchuria, in the northeastern part of today's China, was the home province of the Manchu people, who built the Qing dynasty (1636–1912). The Qing prohibited non-Manchu people from moving into this region, a prohibition that kept the population small and allowed deep forests, vast marshlands, and grasslands to extend across Manchuria. However, as the Qing dynasty's power waned, more people from the mainland China migrated into Manchuria, and in 1870, the rulers were forced to repeal the prohibition. As the population grew, agriculture, including soy cultivation, expanded into what had been wild lands (Zhu 2014; Yasutomi and Fukao eds. 2009). Manchuria became the supplier of soy bean and soy meal to Mainland China.

Some Chinese books on agriculture begin to mention soy meal as fertilizer around the middle of the Qing dynasty (1616–1912), when Chinese farmers near Shanghai were starting to use it to enhance the production of cotton as a cash crop. Around the same time, Chinese traders who shipped food and other products from Southern China to the northern capital on the Grand Canal found soy meal to be a convenient commodity to fill the empty ships heading back south. Later, soy meal was also used to fertilize sugarcane, another cash crop, in the southern regions. Then, the soy meal trade expanded beyond the north–south canal route to the sea coast, coming to include the southern ports of Fujian and Canton. As the Qing dynasty continued to weaken in the 19th century, trade and travel via both canal and coast gradually became deregulated. After the two Opium Wars (1841–1842 and 1856–1860), when the British forced China to open its key ports, including the port of Yingkou (also known as Niuzhuang) in Manchuria, British traders began to ship soy meal from Yingkou to Southern China. More soy-crushing factories were built in the port city, and finally, the export of soy products (bean, oil, and meal) was entirely deregulated in 1868 (Yasutomi and Fukao eds. 2009; Adachi 1978; Sakaguchi 2003; Shaw 1911).

In this way, the cultivation of soy, the beginning of soy-crushing, the use of soy meal as a fertilizer for cash crops, and the domestic trade of soy meal had developed in Manchuria and China by the 19th century. This was the situation when Japan opened its economy and demanded soy meal as fertilizer to modernize its agriculture.

Bibliography

In English

Buck, J. L. (1930) *Chinese Farm Economy: A Study of 2866 Farms in Seventeen Localities and Seven Provinces in China*, The University of Nanking and the China Council of the Institute of Pacific Relations by the University of Chicago.

Rikyu-Hachiman (n.d.) “Legendary Shrine History”, available at: http://rikyuhachiman.org/history.html (accessed February 13, 2024).

Shaw, N. (1911) *Soya Bean of Manchuria*, Statistical Dept. of the Inspectorate General of Customs.

In Japanese (with English translation by the author)

Adachi, K. (1978) “Commercial Farming and the Use of Soybean-Meal Fertilizer in the Ch’ing Dynasty”, *The Journal of Oriental Researches*, 37(3), pp. 361–389. (足立啓二　[1978]「大豆粕流通と清代の商業的農業」東洋史研究　37巻3号 pp. 361–389.)

Hirano, M. and Kobayashi, K. (1976) *The Book of Tempura* (平野正章, 小林菊衛 [1976]『てんぷらの本』柴田書店).

Masuno, M. (1942) *Soybean and Its Industry in the World* (増野實 [1942]『世界の大豆と工業』河出書房).

Ooura, M. and Hirano, S. eds. (1948) *Golden Flower: The History of Japan Oil Company* (大浦万吉・平野茂之 編 [1948]『黄金の花: 日本製油株式会社沿革史（改訂増補版）』新潮社).

Sakaguchi, M. (2003) "The Bean Cake Market of Modern Japan", *Rikkyo Economic Review*, 57(2), pp. 53–70 (坂口誠 [2003]「近代日本の大豆粕市場: 輸入肥料の時代」立教経済学研究 57(2), pp. 53–70).
Sakaguchi, Y. (1987) *My History (Yukio Sakaguchi)* (坂口幸雄 [1987]『坂口幸雄 私の履歴書』日本経済新聞社).
SMR (South Manchuria Railway) (1924a) *On Soy Processing* (南満洲鉄道株式会社農務課 [1924]『大豆の加工』（産業資料 其21）満蒙文化協会。
SMR (South Manchuria Railway) (1924b) *On Oil-press Industry in Manchuria* (南満州鉄道株式会社庶務部調査課 [1924] 『滿洲に於ける油坊業』（滿鐵調査資料 第23編）南滿洲鐵道株式會社庶務部調査課).
Yasutomi, A. and Fukao, Y. eds. (2009) *"Manchuria" Loss of Forest and Formation of Modern Space* (安冨歩・深尾葉子 編 [2009] 『「満洲」の成立: 森林の消尽と近代空間の形成』名古屋大学出版会).
Zhu, M. (2014) "Japanese Oil Companies Expansion to Manchuria from the Beginning of 20th Century to the End of WW2" (朱美栄「20世紀初頭から第2次世界大戦終結に至るまでの日系製油企業の満洲進出とその展開: 日清製油を中心に」学位論文（博士）愛知淑徳大学 2014年).

Website

NDL Digital Collections https://dl.ndl.go.jp/en/, National Diet Library (Japan).

2 Importing Manchurian soy meal as fertilizer (19th century to WWI)

Japan's state-building project and the birth of the modern soy-industry

Introduction

Around the end of the 19th century, Japan began importing large amounts of soy meal, and Japanese companies turned to building factories in Manchuria, where they mass-produced soy meal as fertilizer for Japanese agriculture and soy oil as an export commodity for the United States and European countries. Soy-crushing soon became a capital-intensive mechanical-industry, with powered machinery and solvent-extraction facilities. The financial-mercantile-industrial capital of *zaibatsu* and their trading sectors that functioned as traders for the government promoted the development of a modern soy-industry in both Manchuria and Japan, with the active support of the Japanese government as a state-building project to accumulate capital in Japanese hands and to expand their political and economic influence in Asia. Again, it is important to note that this development of the soy-industry and the trade of soy products was not to feed people, but a means for the Japanese government and businesses to quickly gain power in the capitalist world-economy while resisting Western colonization. In the process, soy was transformed from a traditional Asian food into a global commodity.

Japan's increasing demand for purchased fertilizer

Japan had established an almost self-sufficient economy during its national seclusion from the beginning of the 17th century to the middle of the 19th century. Japanese farmers had achieved nearly sustainable soil management practices with little input from outside, although they suffered from heavy government duties paid in rice, other commodities, or labor. After Japan opened up, however, the Meiji government promoted a new "Meiji farming method" that used more animal power and purchased fertilizer inputs, aiming to modernize agriculture and rural communities (Ushiyama 2008). Fishmeal from Japan's northern sea was used at first, but the supply

DOI: 10.4324/9781032678733-3

was limited. Chemical fertilizer was not yet produced domestically, so it was expensive. At that time, soy meal from Manchuria was introduced as purchased fertilizer. It is said that a small amount of soy meal was already being imported from Manchuria around the 1890s (Nisshin Oil 1969, 53), and Chinese traders in Yokohama had also brought some soy meal from Manchuria to Japan (SMR 1924b). While various historical sources record slightly different stories of the beginning of the soy meal trade to Japan, exports from Manchuria of soy meal for fertilizer drastically increased from the end of the 19th century.

Japan's state-building and Manchurian soy

Before further exploring the development of soy-industry in Manchuria, this section explains some background of Japanese political economy; why modernizing Japanese government, financial institutions, *zaibatsu* and their trading sectors, saw opportunity in this soy meal fertilizer business for their state-building project. After Japan opened its secluded country and began modernizing, and especially after the Meiji Restoration of 1868, Japanese leaders were desperate to avoid the invasion of Western traders and capital into domestic markets and to hurry Japan's industrial development. To do that, Japan quickly modernized its financial and industrial institutions and tried to accumulate capital in Japanese hands by expanding into other parts of Asia and developing international trade.

The national government: Resisting Western colonization

During the era of national isolation, while international trade was strictly limited and controlled under the monopoly of the feudal government, domestic trade flourished, and Japanese traders and financial institutions developed inside the country. Strong trade routes were established between Western Japan, with Osaka (the center of commerce) and Kyoto (the traditional capital where the emperors lived), and Eastern Japan, with Edo (today's Tokyo, the political center). Each feudal province developed specialty commodities and traded them to finance their clans. Maritime trade routes also developed in the inland seas and inshore waterways around the Japanese archipelago. Japanese traders handled a wide variety of commodities and products, as well as the domestic financial exchange of gold, silver, and copper.

Then, in the middle of the 19th century, Western delegates came to demand that Japan open its markets. Japan agreed to the Japan–US Amity Treaty in 1854, and then to the Friendship and Trade Treaty with Britain, France, the Netherlands, and Russia in 1858. The treaties forced Japan to renounce its tariff autonomy and consular jurisdiction, and they approved the most-favored-nation treatment of these countries. Although Japan accepted these unfair trade agreements with the Western countries, both the Edo feudal government and the newly established Meiji government insisted on limiting foreign trade and residence to designated "settlements" (*kyoryuchi*居留地) in specified port towns like Yokohama and Kobe. The Japanese thus tried their best to keep foreign traders and foreign capital from entering Japan (Ishii 2005, 2).

Just announcing such a policy might not have worked in the unbalanced global power context at the height of Western colonialism. However, the relatively well-established Japanese domestic economy and its accumulated wealth allowed Japan to impose some actual limitations on the Western traders and capital entering its domestic markets. The established domestic traders, led by feudal-era merchants and moneylenders, including Mitsui and Sumitomo, and newly grown entrepreneurs like IWASAKI Yataro (the founder of Mitsubishi), OKURA Kihachiro, and Suzuki Shoten, worked as the Japanese counterparts of the Western traders, dealing with them in the settlements and thus avoiding any foreign presence in the rest of Japan. This "settlement trading" was very competitive and a risky business for Japanese traders, yet it also offered an opportunity for some to rapidly develop and accumulate capital. This is regarded as one of the reasons Japan was able to avoid Western colonization and accomplish its own industrial revolution as almost the only such case among Asian countries (Ishii 2005, 2012). While keeping the Western powers at bay, Japan quickly modernized its financial institutions and trading systems.

The banks: Modernizing Japanese financial institutions to secure capital in Japanese hands

The Japanese government believed that Western investment and the entry of financial institutions into the country was a step toward colonization, so it tried to modernize Japan's financial systems in order to keep capital in Japanese hands. The situation was serious. The unfair trade treaties and the exchange rate between gold and silver in Japan, which was different from the international rate, initially allowed a large amount of gold to be drained away. The Meiji government had to move quickly to develop Japanese financial institutions to counter the foreign institutions.

During the era of Japan's isolation, multiple domestic currencies of gold, silver, and copper were used for domestic trade, and a domestic currency exchange system and financial institutions had existed since the feudal era. With this background, the Japanese government was able to organize new legal frameworks for a modern national banking system in the 1870s (Oishi and Miyamoto eds. 1975). To secure control over foreign currency exchange and international trade settlements, the government founded

Yokohama Specie Bank (YSB, 横浜正金銀行, one of the origins of today's Bank of Tokyo-Mitsubishi UFJ) in 1880, and also established the Bank of Japan as the central bank in 1882. Thus, Japan's modern financial system was established within a few decades of the opening of its economy, and the capital that accumulated in Japanese hands was available to invest in Japan's industrial revolution (Ishii 2012, 61). YSB played an especially significant role as the special bank to manage international trade settlements and to secure specie money (gold and silver in those days) in Japan, competing against foreign banks and supporting the financing of the government's public budget. It soon broadened its role, developing international trade for Japan and helping Japanese traders expand overseas, especially in the surrounding Asian regions. Manchuria was one of the earliest targets for such expansion（Hijikata 1980; Ishii 2012, 61; Kiyama 2009, 235–236).

Zaibatsu *and "government traders"*

Japan needed its own strong traders. The Western traders were expanding into Asia with threatening power, and Indian and Chinese traders were also active in trade and commerce in the Asian region in those days (Sugihara 1996). Japan wanted to finance industrial development and to implement the policies encapsulated in the slogan "increase wealth and military power" (富国強兵). Because the country had to import machinery and raw materials (e.g., textile and other industrial machines, steel, iron ore, cotton, etc.), it had to export whatever products it could sell to the world market to obtain foreign currency. The Japanese government therefore turned to existing rich family groups like Mitsui and Sumitomo, as well as newly developed groups like Mitsubishi and Okura, to handle international trade and to develop key industries. They were called *seisho* (政商), which literally means "government traders." As the name indicates, they received special support from the Meiji government and conducted the government's business with that authority, when Japan began its industrial and capitalist development at the end of the 19th century (Oishi and Miyamoto eds. 1975).

The birth of the Mitsui zaibatsu *and Mitsui&Co.*

The Mitsui family began trading kimono and currencies during the feudal era. They opened a store to sell high-quality kimono from Kyoto in the capital city of Edo in the middle of the 17th century. In those days, the Japanese domestic currency system was complicated, with gold-, silver-, and copper-based currencies issued by multiple authorities in different districts, so Mitsui also conducted money exchange to settle payments for long-distance trade. They also handled the budget of the feudal authority (*bakufu*) and lent some money to feudal lords. Although Mitsui separated their kimono business (which later became the Mitsukoshi department store) when they transformed into a modern business group, their solid foundation in domestic trade and financial systems since the feudal era was why Mitsui was strong enough to become a partner of the Meiji government (Morikawa 1978; Shibagaki 1968).

Mitsui&Co., the trading company of the Mitsui *zaibatsu* group, had strong connections to the national government from the start; it was incorporated in 1876 as the Mitsui family took over a trading company from INOUE Kaoru, a cabinet member and key figure in the Meiji government (Japan Business History Institute 1976). The next year, it opened a branch office in Shanghai, at the government's request, to handle a loan to the Chinese government to sell Japanese coal (Kiyama 2009, 75). Mitsui handled the government's finances and collected taxes, while expanding overseas trade and investing in various key industries. By the time of the Russo-Japanese War (1904–1905), Mitsui&Co. was handling up to 20% of Japan's international trade and was so powerful that it was called the de facto "Trading Department of Japan, Inc." (Kasuga 2010, 1; Sakamoto 2003). When Mitsui&Co. went to Manchuria as part of the national policy of expansion and to look for new business opportunities, the domestic soy-industry was just beginning to grow there, and Mitsui&Co. became a pioneer in the trade of Manchuria soy products to Japan and the world.

The birth of the Mitsubishi zaibatsu *and Mitsubishi Corporation*

Unlike Mitsui or Sumitomo, which had their origins in the feudal era, the Mitsubishi *zaibatsu* was formed by an entrepreneur and nationalist, IWASAKI Yataro, in the 1870s. Early on, Mitsubishi established itself in marine transport for domestic trading. It later became a military transport company, building strong connections with the national government and helping the government suppress rebellions in Western Japan and taking soldiers to Taiwan in the 1870s.

The Japanese government asked Mitsubishi to open a regular marine transport route between Japan and Shanghai in 1875, and it was also Mitsubishi that opened the first regular marine transport route between Japan and the Manchurian port of Yingkou in the 1890s. The Japanese government supported Mitsubishi because it wanted to secure these routes under Japanese control against the threat of US and UK shipping companies that were moving into Asia at the time. In this way, Mitsubishi became one of the government traders as the major shipping and trading company, both domestic and international, and for both commercial and military purposes. Eventually, Mitsubishi diversified into mining, ship-building, and other key industries, growing into one of the biggest *zaibatsu* of Japan.

It also developed its trading sector and a financial institution, which later incorporated as Mitsubishi Corporation and Mitsubishi Bank, respectively (Mishima 1979; Shibagaki 1968).

In summary, the newly established Japanese government was desperate to modernize the Japanese economy quickly to avoid Western colonization. While the government restricted foreign traders and their capital from coming into Japan, Japanese *zaibatsu* families and their trading sectors gained power, taking advantage of their role as the intermediaries handling domestic trade for the foreigners. They developed trading systems and key industries with the support of the government (Ishii 2012). Mitsui and Mitsubishi received particular support from the Department of the Interior and the Department of Finance, respectively. In order to boost industrial development as a latecomer to the capitalist world-economy, the Japanese government first built government enterprises in key sectors, including transportation and mining (gold, silver, and coal), as well as both light industries (silk and cotton textiles) and heavy industries (steel and military equipment). Then, about a decade later, these government enterprises were given to private companies, many of them *zaibatsu* groups, including Mitsui and Mitsubishi, to accelerate Japan's industrial development. This government-led development strategy gave an enormous advantage to the *zaibatsu* and their related companies, which rapidly became significant components of the Japanese economy (Kasuga 2010, 4; Oishi and Miyamoto 1975, 39).

Expansion to Manchuria and the development of the soy-industry and global trade

Just before Japan began expanding to the Asian continent, China and Manchuria were also opened by Western forces. In Manchuria, the British opened the port of Yingkou in 1861. The Japanese government built a consulate there in 1876; the Nippon Yusen (of Mitsubishi group) began regular shipping services between Yingkou and Japan in 1890; Mitsui&Co. opened their own office there in the early 1890s; and YSB opened a branch office in Yingkou in 1900 (Kaneko 1991, 28; Nisshin Oil 1969, 18). In this way, the government, its special bank, and its favored traders together expanded into key cities of Manchuria as the leading "trinity" of Japan's overseas expansion (Kasuga 2010, 1). When these Japanese players had laid the groundwork for international trade between Manchuria and Japan, as well as the rest of the world, they were ready to seize the business opportunities offered by Manchuria's soy meal production and Japan's fertilizer demand. Their handling of Manchurian soy not only supported the development of the soy-industry in Manchuria but also triggered the international trade of soy products, including meal and oil, from Manchuria.

As Chapter 1 described, some soy meal had already been being shipped out from Manchuria, but the trade had been limited to the coastal ports of Southern China. Then, in the 1890s, Japan became the major export destination beyond the Chinese continent. As trade statistics show (Table 2.1), the export of soy meal to Japan increased rapidly, until Japan accounted for 100% of Manchurian soy meal exports in the year 1892 (Kaneko 1991, 23). These exports accelerated after the first Sino-Japanese War (1894–1895). Manchurian soy "expanded from domestic trade inside of China, into international trade toward East Asian countries" (Kaneko 1991, 24), starting with the export of soy meal to Japan.

Manchurian soy and the South Manchuria Railway as a colonial institution

With victory in the Russo-Japanese War of 1904–1905, Japan's reach in Asia expanded to Korea, Manchuria, and other parts of China. The Treaty of Portsmouth gave Japan Russia's rights and leases in Port Arthur (旅順) and Dalian (大連), strategically important ports on the Liaodong (遼東) peninsula, as well as the rights to part of the Chinese Eastern Railway (東清鉄道) between Changchun and Port Arthur. With these gains, Japan began its full-scale imperial expansion to Asia. The Japanese government aimed to establish a division of labor in which its territories of Taiwan, Korea, and Manchuria would supply the agricultural products and raw materials required for Japan's industrial development, while Japan would export its manufactured products (mainly textiles) to these territories and to the world. Sugar and rice were imported from Taiwan, mainly by the government traders, including Mitsui&Co. and Mitsubishi Corporation. The railway in Korea played an important role by transporting agricultural products, including rice and soy, from inland areas of the Korean peninsula to ports for shipment to Japan, and transporting Japanese textile products back to the Korean market. The Japanese government politically and financially supported its special banks, including YSB, the Taiwan Bank, and the Korean Bank, as well as transport companies in shipping and railways (Japan nationalized its domestic railways around the same time), and continued working closely with the *zaibatsu* groups (Oishi and Miyamoto 1975).

In order to manage its newly acquired territory in Manchuria, Japan stationed a unit of the Imperial Japanese Army, the Guandong Army (関東軍), there in 1906, and established the South Manchuria Railway Co., Ltd. (SMR) by government order in 1906. SMR was a "national policy corporation" (国策会社), making it a semiofficial organization with the aim of implementing Japan's national policies of expansion in Asia (Figure 2.1).

Despite its name, the SMR was far more than an ordinary railway company; some scholars called it "the East India Corporation of Japan" (Kasuga 2010). Although it took the form of a limited liability company, half of

Table 2.1 Trade from the Manchurian port of Yingkou before the Russo-Japanese War, 1872–1904, and export destinations, 1891–1904 (unit: money value 1000 haikwan taels, %)

Trade from Yingkou (includes indirect export via inland China ports)				*Destination of direct export*				
	Total export	*Soy products (bean, oil, meal)*	*% of soy products*	*To Japan*	*% of Japan*	*To Hong Kong*	*To UK*	*Total*
1872	2,001	1,740	**87.0%**					
1873	1,582	1,254	**79.3%**					
1874	1,754	1,374	**78.3%**					
1875	2,688	2,215	**82.4%**					
1876	2,639	2,090	**79.2%**					
1877	3,130	2,389	**76.3%**					
1878	4,387	3,511	**80.0%**					
1879	3,655	3,152	**86.2%**					
1880	3,353	2,719	**81.1%**					
1881	3,552	2,802	**78.9%**					
1882	3,626	2,961	**81.7%**					
1883	3,913	3,242	**82.9%**					
1884	4,123	3,282	**79.6%**					
1885	4,574	3,577	**78.2%**					
1886	4,527	3,136	**69.3%**					
1887	5,477	4,008	**73.2%**					
1888	5,686	4,358	**76.6%**					
1889	5,568	3,987	**71.6%**					
1890	7,198	5,070	**70.4%**					
				To Japan	*% of Japan*	*To Hong Kong*	*To UK*	*Total*
1891	8,070	6,363	**78.8%**	460	**99.8%**			461
1892	9,066	6,496	**71.7%**	1,173	**100.0%**			1,173
1893	9,310	7,065	**75.9%**	1,732	79.9%	433	0	2,167
1894	8,532	6,676	**78.2%**	1,129	84.6%	181	0	1,335
1895	5,605	4,579	**81.7%**	54	9.8%	441		550
1896	11,277	9,455	**83.8%**	3,104	87.3%	433	1	3,556
1897	13,809	11,373	**82.4%**	5,114	92.2%	414	9	5,548
1898	17,448	14,075	**80.7%**	6,683	93.1%	433	5	7,179
1899	20,616	16,686	**80.9%**	8,092	93.1%	589	0	8,691
1900	11,470	9,643	**84.1%**	3,458	88.6%	426	3	3,905
1901	18,742	16,089	**85.8%**	6,562	89.9%	597	1	7,303
1902	17,525	14,314	**81.7%**	8,019	91.8%	604	2	8,733
1903	19,982	14,636	**73.2%**	9,374	92.1%	695	13	10,179
1904	12,159	8,751	**72.0%**	1,084	69.0%	449	38	1,571

Source: Adapted from Kaneko (1991, 22–23).

Note: Bold values are emphasis by the author.

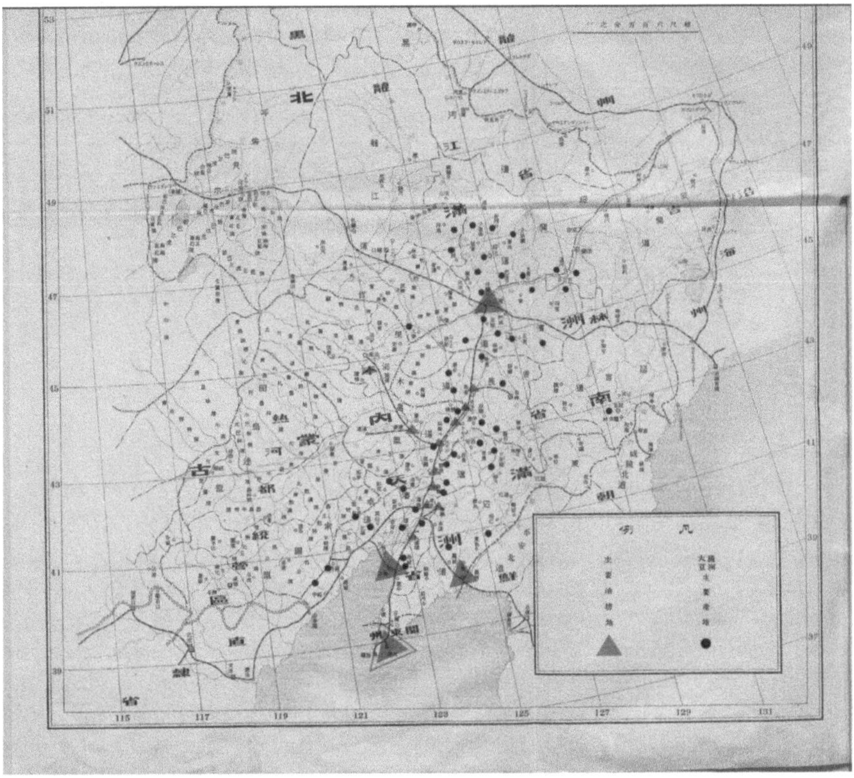

Figure 2.1 Map of Manchuria, showing major soy production sites (circles), major soy-crushing sites (gray triangles), and the railway routes linking them. Date of the map not specified.

Source: Adapted from SMR (1924b, 35).

its funding came from the government, and its founding board members consisted of officials from the government, special banks including YSB, and Mitsui&Co. (Kaneko 1991, 88). SMR was, in fact, a Japanese colonial institution with the main aim of executing Japan's colonizing projects, rather than simply seeking business profits.

Nevertheless, SMR needed to conduct some railway business to support itself. Its profits came from cargo transportation, especially at the beginning. An analysis by the Japanese historian KANEKO Fumio found that the transport of soy products accounted for about 40% of SMR's cargo transport profits, with a peak of 57.4% in 1908 (Table 2.2). This was much more than the proportion of its profit from transporting coal (less than 10%

Table 2.2 SMR's profits from cargo transport of soy meal and coal, 1907–1914 (unit: %)

	Ordinary cargo		*Cargo for company business*	
	Soy meal	*Others*	*Coal*	*Others*
1907	37.3	45.4	4.1	13.2
1908	57.4	28.4	8.1	6.2
1909	48.6	33.0	11.1	7.3
1910	48.8	33.2	12.8	6.1
1911	43.4	35.6	15.4	5.6
1912	38.1	36.9	21.4	3.6
1913	35.9	33.2	26.5	4.4
1914	44.9	29.9	23.0	2.2

Source: Adapted from Kaneko (1991, 106).

until 1908). SMR eventually diversified its business to some extent, but soy products (beans, meal, and oil) continued to account for about 40% of its transport profits until WWI (Kaneko 1991, 106). In this way, soy-related business contributed to the stable development of SMR, thereby supporting Japan's colonial operations in Manchuria (Kaneko 1991, 106–107).

Both the Japanese government and SMR fully acknowledged the importance of the soy-industry and international trade of soy products for their colonial occupation of Manchuria. They actively developed the soy-crushing industry and facilitated more efficient trading and transport systems for the large-scale export of Manchurian soy products, with Dalian at the center. SMR's activities related to the Manchurian soy-industry included:

- Heavily investing in transport facilities around the railway network, expanding port facilities, building storage warehouses and hotels, and increasing rail and ship transport capacity, so as to increase soy product exports via Dalian. Mitsui&Co. handled a large part of the purchase of train cars and construction materials for SMR.
- Reorganizing the trade route of Manchurian soy products via the port in Dalian, rather than the previously developed trade route via Yingkou. One of its actions was setting an advantageous fee for Manchurian soy products to be transported by SMR and exported from the port in Dalian.
- Contributing to organizing a more efficient trading system, and providing quality control by blending and inspecting soy products, thus securing uniform and stable quality for bulk trade in the global market. SMR also began a warehouse business and an insurance system.

In this way, SMR contributed to facilitating the large-scale trade of standardized soy products as an industrial ingredient for export to the world market (Kaneko 1991; Nakajima ed. 1967; Manshi-kai 1964).

As the postcards in Figure 2.2 show, Japan established the railway cargo link of SMR to the Dalian port, which was connected to marine transport routes to Japan. Manchurian soy products—bean, meal, and oil—became the major commodities for this business and for the benefit of Japanese big business, colonial institutions, and government.

Based on this study, I argue that Japanese colonial policies and SMR's work promoted the development of Manchuria's soy-industry and international trade of their soy products, while enforcing the Japanese colonial occupation at the same time. Regardless of whether its purpose was political or economic, the Japanese colonial institution of the SMR contributed to soy becoming a globally traded commodity and to Manchuria becoming the center of the world soy export trade by the 1930s.

Parallel to SMR establishing its colonial foothold in Manchuria, these favorable conditions for Japanese capital—with public order protected by the Japanese military, the presence of Japanese trading and financial institutions organized by the state and *zaibatsu*, the promotion of the soy business by the South Manchuria Railway, and the established trade routes to Japan and the world market—encouraged more Japanese investment in the Manchurian soy-industry, with the port of Dalian as the center of the Manchurian soy economy (Nisshin Oil 1969, 24).

Nisshin Oil: The company founded by the Okura zaibatsu *and a fertilizer broker*

Seeing the rapid increase of soy meal imports from Manchuria, Japanese *zaibatsu* and other companies decided to enter the soy-crushing business and trade themselves. In 1907, the Okura *zaibatsu*, which was aiming to expand into Manchuria, and a Japanese fertilizer broker, came together to found a company that became the dominant oil company in Japan today: Nisshin OilliO Group (Nisshin Oil, hereafter).

The Okura *zaibatsu* may be little known today, with their business limited to certain industries like hotels and construction. However, at the beginning of the Meiji era of modernization, the Okura *zaibatsu* group was quite influential as a typical government trader (*seisho zaibatsu*), working with and for the national government. In particular, the Okura *zaibatsu* worked for the military by handling arms trading and played a key role in Japan's Asia expansion policy. Okura was involved in the Sino-Japanese War (1894–1895), the Russo-Japanese War (1904–1905), and WWI. The group was started by OKURA Kihachiro, who was born in 1837. Okura began a dry goods business in Edo, but soon turned to trading guns and

(a)

(b)

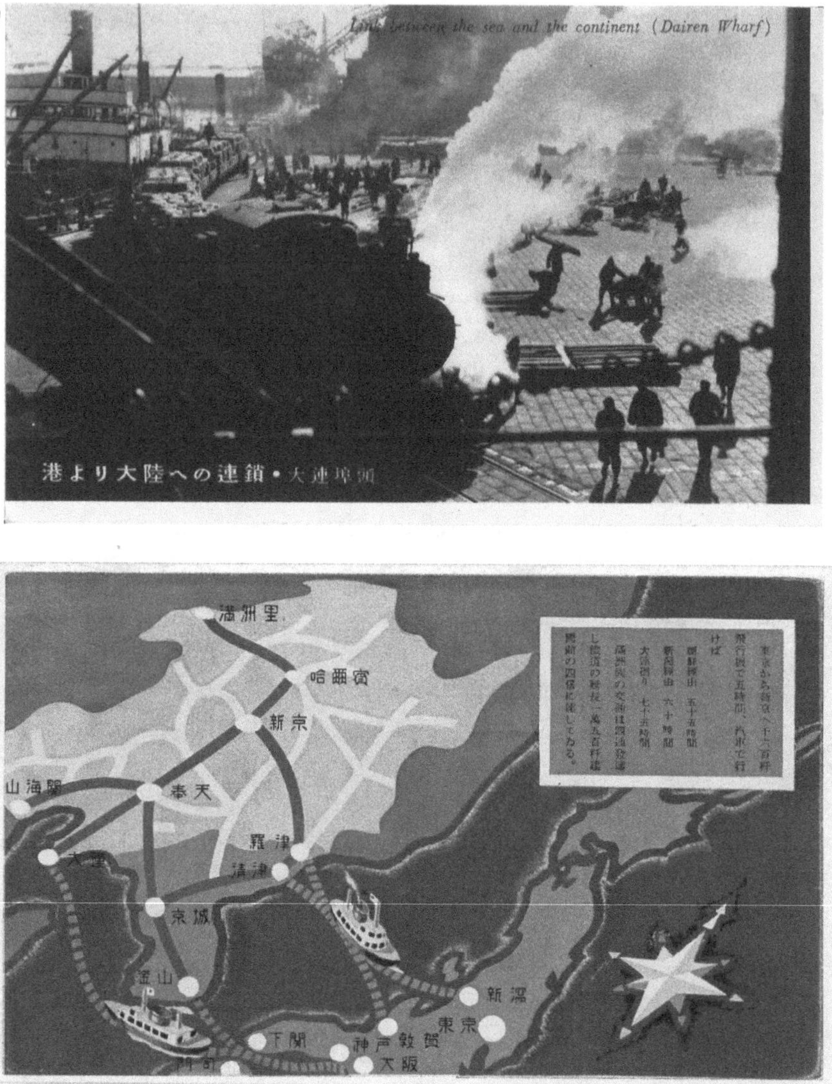

Figure 2.2 Postcards that show an SMR train in Dalian port (a) and the SMR and marine transport routes linking Manchuria and Japan (b). (Photograph courtesy of the Main Library, Kyoto University Rare Materials Digital Archive "Asia Depicted on Postcards", https://rmda.kulib.kyoto-u.ac.jp/en/collection/asia-pc).

(a) "Link between the Sea and the Continent (Dairen Wharf) [sic]," n.d.; (b) "Traffic Map between Japan and Manchukuo," 1942.

munitions. He traveled to Europe in 1872 and made connections with the members of the Iwakura diplomatic mission visiting there. Such personal connections with key people in the Japanese government contributed to the Okura *zaibatsu* becoming a government trader (Okura Zaibatsu Research Association 1982).

Around the same time, the fertilizer broker MATSUSHITA Kyujiro began importing Manchurian soy meal to replace fishmeal. He moved his office from the traditional center of Japan's fertilizer business to the port city of Yokohama, for the convenience of importing soy meal (Nisshin Oil 1969, 53). Around the time of the Sino-Japanese War (1894–1895), when Japan achieved the first step of its industrial revolution (mainly in light industry), the demand for soy meal for fertilizer increased rapidly. Matsushita became a significant player in the fertilizer industry, and he caught the attention of the Okura group.

Thus, the Okura *zaibatsu*, which was deeply involved in the military and expansion policies of Japan, and the fertilizer broker, who imported Manchurian soy meal, joined hands and established a new company in 1907, the origin of today's dominant edible oil company, Nisshin OilliO Group. The founding board members included relatives and business partners of OKURA Kihachiro, indicating the strong position of the *zaibatsu* group in the new company (Nisshin Oil 1969, 5–7). The original company name was *Nisshin Mame-kasu Seizou Kabushikigaisha* (日清豆粕製造株式会社), which literally means "Japan-China Bean Meal Manufacturing Company," reflecting the main product of the day being soy meal rather than soy oil. The corporate history says that "soy bean oil was little utilized for edible purposes in those days. Oil was a by-product. The main use of soy bean was to manufacture soy meal rather than to extract oil" (Nisshin Oil 1969, 5).

Nisshin Oil was incorporated in Tokyo, but the first thing the company did was to open an office in Yingkou and build a factory in Dalian, both in Manchuria. The executive board members frequently traveled to Manchuria, and they negotiated with the Japanese army there to rent land for their factory, which was connected to the SMR and the Dalian port. The factory was completed at the end of 1907, and it began test operations in August the following year. After that, Nisshin Oil remained a dominant company in the Manchurian soy-industry until the end of WWII (Nisshin Oil 1969, 16–17; Zhu 2014).

Next to the Nisshin Oil factory in Dalian, Mitsui&Co. and local capital jointly built another soy-crushing company (三泰油房). By then, Mitsui&Co., which had already been trading Manchurian soy meal to Japan, was thoroughly entwined in SMR's projects and Manchuria's economy.

The privatization of a colonial innovation: The origin of the Honen Oil group

While promoting trade via Dalian as a railroad company, SMR also built top-level R&D sections to find available resources in Manchuria and develop the related industries to maximize these resources for the benefit of Japan. The Research Section of SMR (満鉄調査部) was established in 1907 as a think tank to support the Japanese colonization. Top researchers from the imperial universities of Japan were invited to work there. In addition to studying the social and economic situation of Manchuria, they actively studied the production and industrial possibilities of agricultural resources in Manchuria, including wheat, sugar, animal products, and, of course, soy. Especially, the SMR Central Laboratory (満鉄中央試験所), which was reorganized by merging with military laboratory in 1910, conducted four decades of research, some of which was purely academic, but most of it was practical research to develop industries and businesses based on the resources available in Manchuria (Manshikai 1964, 577; Sugita 1995).

Because the development of the soy-industry contributed to SMR, and thus to Japan, the SMR Central Laboratory had great interest in improving the soy-industry there. It researched soy varieties with higher oil content, developed more efficient technologies for oil extraction, and found new industrial products that could be made from soy oil and soy meal (Kikuchi 1994, 70). With the ample capital and elite human resources available to it as a national policy company, SMR investigated in cutting-edge technologies for oil-press machinery and oil-extraction methods, especially focusing on a solvent-extraction method using benzine. The SMR Central Laboratory obtained this technology from Germany and built the SMR Soy Oil Manufactory, which began test production in 1915. Then, the technology and the facilities were given to Suzuki Shoten, the largest *zaibatsu* of the time.

Suzuki Shoten is sometimes called an illusionary *sogo-shosha* (Suzukishoten-museum 2014). Although it is little known even among Japanese people, Suzuki Shoten ranked alongside Mitsui and Mitsubishi around the beginning of the 20th century. By 1902, it had overseas offices in London, Hamburg, and New York, and by 1917, its sales made up about 10% of Japan's GDP. The Suzuki family began trading imported sugar in Kobe, one of the settlements for foreigners, around the 1870s. The company found success in settlement trading, and rapidly grew, expanding from sugar to camphor, celluloid, steel, leather, tobacco, alcohol, as well as soy and fish oils. It also began manufacturing hardened oil from these oil resources. Suzuki Shoten invested in many companies in key industries inside and around Japan. After going bankrupt in 1927, Suzuki Shoten disappeared from history, with its corporate records scattered and remained little researched. Its legacy remains, however, in dozens of major companies to this day, including in the steel and heavy machinery, petrol chemical, marine transport, general trading, and food and beverage sectors.

SMR's cutting-edge solvent-extraction facilities became Suzuki Shoten's Oil Section, which in 1922 was incorporated into Honen Oil Company, one of the origins of the other dominant oil company in Japan today, J-Oil Mills. After acquiring SMR's oil-extraction factory in Dalian, Suzuki Shoten expanded its production capacity. It also built more solvent-extraction factories inside of Japan, in Shimizu, Naruo, and Yokohama—all in port districts that featured convenient access to imported soy from Manchuria and to shipping out the finished products (Honen Oil 1944, 40). Suzuki Shoten was very active in international trade, dealing with a wide range of products. It became the best-known Japanese trader in London and made huge profits during WWI. However, when the postwar economic turmoil began in the 1920s, Suzuki Shoten faced severe difficulties. In its restructuring efforts, the vegetable oil sectors of Suzuki Shoten were cut off, and a new company, Honen Oil, was incorporated in 1922, succeeding to the factories in Dalian and Japan. Suzuki Shoten continued to struggle due to economic and political conflicts and finally became bankrupt during Japan's financial panic of 1927 (Honen Oil 1944; Katsura 1976).

The development of the Japanese soy-industry with imported Manchurian soy

In addition to these *zaibatsu*-related major companies, some smaller-scale soy-crushing factories were built in Japan, also crushed imported Manchurian soy bean. According to *Golden Flower*'s history of the Japanese vegetable oil industries, the first soy-crushing factory in Japan was built in 1902 in Tsuruga, a port city facing the Asian continent, in today's Fukui prefecture. The companies that began crushing soy in those days had "soy meal" in their company names rather than "oil" or "refinery," indicating that the meal was their main product. These factories were built on the coasts, giving them easy access to the ports, and from the start they used imported Manchurian soy as their raw material, rather than depending on domestic production, although Japanese farmers had been growing soy for centuries (Ooura and Hirano eds. 1948).

As more factories began crushing soy beans and producing soy meal in Japan, the government encouraged the development of this domestic soy-crushing industry. In 1906, the government made various tariff adjustments to make importing Manchurian soy bean favorable relative to importing Manchurian soy meal. In 1912, the government more or less abandoned tariffs on whole soy bean imports to some designated ports, including Yokohama and Kobe, as well as other port areas in Aichi, Mie, and Sizuoka prefectures (Ooura and Hirano eds. 1948; Masuno 1942; Honen Oil

1944). These government policies encouraged the building of more soy-crushing factories in Japan, especially in the port districts.

The *zaibatsu* also turned to building domestic factories, and they rapidly increased production capacity in Japan by investing in large-scale manufacturing with new technologies and machineries. Suzuki Shoten, which had inherited the solvent-extraction technology from SMR in Dalian, introduced this technology to Japan and built three more solvent-extraction factories in Shimizu, Naruo, and Yokohama—all in port districts that featured convenient access to imported soy beans from Manchuria (Honen Oil 1944, 40). With the outbreak of WWI, world demand for oils and fats surged. The war led to both the withdrawal of European forces from Asia and an enormous increase in soy oil demand, thus creating a "golden era" for the Japanese soy-crushing industry. Suzuki Shoten regarded WWI as "heaven's blessing" because the *zaibatsu*'s soy-related business received huge orders from many countries (Honen Oil 1944, 26; Nisshin Oil 1969, 4).

Table 2.3 shows the soy-crushing factories in Japan around 1918 that had a production capacity of more than 100 tons per day and their production methods (oil-press or solvent-extraction).

This "golden era" of the soy-crushing industry, and the rapid increase of soy meal and soy oil production in Japan, came *before* the Japanese people began eating soy oil. Almost all of the soy oil being produced was exported, mainly to Western countries.

Table 2.3 Large-scale soy-crushing factories (daily crushing capacity of more than 100 tons) in Japan around 1918

Factory name	*Location*	*Methods*	*Daily soy-crushing capacity (ton)*
Matsushita Soy meal Manufacturing (Nisshin Oil)	Yokohama (Kanagawa)	Press	120
Yokohama Soy meal Manufacturing	Yokohama (Kanagawa)	Press	100
Suzuki Shoten Oil Section (Honen Oil)	Yokohama (Kanagawa)	Solvent extraction	150
Suzuki Shoten Oil Section (Honen Oil)	Shimizu (Shizuoka)	Solvent extraction	300
Yano Oil Refinery	Atsuta (Aichi)	Solvent extraction	100
Suzuki Shoten Oil Section (Honen Oil)	Naruo (Hyogo)	Solvent extraction	200
Nikka Oil	Wakamatsu (Fukuoka)	Solvent extraction	100

Source: Compiled by the author based on data in Masuno (1942, 174–176).

Soy products become global commodities

Soy is known as an oilseed in the West, although it contains much more protein than oil. The origin of this labeling can be traced back to the export of soy oil to the Western countries around the beginning of the 20th century. It is said that soy oil was first introduced to the United Kingdom in 1908, when Mitsui&Co. made a trial shipment to Liverpool, and the British company Lever Brothers soon began to use soy oil for soap manufacturing (Shaw 1911). Special orders from European countries and the United States skyrocketed with WWI, hugely increasing soy oil exports from Manchuria and Japan to the West, as shown by Japanese trade data. An American report, the USDA Statistical Bulletin, also recorded the surge in soy oil imports, from 21 million pounds in 1915 to 145 million the next year and reaching its height at 336 million in 1918 (USDA 1937, 15). This rapid increase in the soy oil trade caught the attention of Western businesses, and some US cottonseed oil mills began crushing imported soy. Soy oil production in the United States was first officially recorded in 1922, with the amount of 751,000 pounds (Eisenschiml 1929), but it was not until the 1930s that domestic soy oil production, as well as soy cultivation, became widespread (Berlan et al. 1977). Europe also imported large amounts of soy bean from the latter half of the 1920s. Germany, which had suffered from an embargo of oil imports during WWI, encouraged the development of a domestic soy-crushing industry and promoted soy bean importation from Manchuria in the 1920s in order to produce its own oil (Hori 2009, 116; Usui 2010, 40; Prodöhl 2023).

Various trade statistics show distinct trade patterns of the Manchurian soy trade, in which soy meal was exported to Japan, soy oil to the West, and soy bean to both Japan and Europe (especially after the 1920s).

Figure 2.3 shows the export destinations of soy products from the three Manchurian ports of Dalian, Yingkou, and Andong in 1930. These data were reported by the SMR in the *North China Trade Bulletin*. Japan was the largest export destination of soy meal, accounting for 60%, but there was almost no export of soy oil to Japan. Soy oil was mainly exported to the United Kingdom and the Netherlands, a gateway to the rest of Europe. The raw material of soy bean was exported to Japan and the Western countries, indicating that the soy-crushing industries had developed in these countries by that time.

Another set of trade data, compiled by the national statistical office of Manchukuo, the puppet-state of Japan, in 1941, shows the same pattern, as represented in the graphs in Figures 2.4 to 2.6, which cover from 1912 to 1938. The accompanying maps illustrate the soy trade situation of 1938.

As Figure 2.4 shows, soy meal was mainly exported to Japan, with some going to other parts of China. Next, Figure 2.5 shows the sharp increase

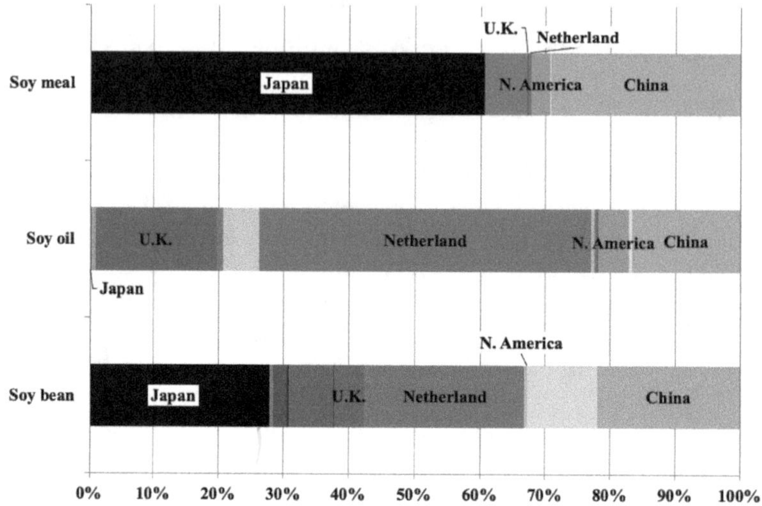

Figure 2.3 The export destinations of soy meal, oil, and bean in 1930 from three major ports of Manchuria (Dalian, Yingkou, and Andong).

Source: Compiled by the author, based on data in SMR (1930, 17–22).

of soy oil exports to the United States in 1917, and then a drop soon after the end of WWI, as well as some postwar increase in soy oil exports to Europe. Later in the 1920s, however, European countries began importing soy bean, as reflected in Figure 2.6, demonstrating that they now had the capacity to process this raw material domestically.

The trade statistics in those days, especially those of soy oil, are confusing, and sometimes show unrealistic figures. Even the Manchukuo statistical officers leave a few figures out, omitting them from the charts. Still, other sets of trade statistics from the era, produced by oil companies or other researchers, show similar patterns and provide enough evidence to argue that modernizing Japan developed the soy-industry for soy meal fertilizer. Contrary to prior explanations that the increase of soy imports to Japan occurred in response to consumer demand, the Japanese soy-industry was not developed because the Japanese people were eating more soy foods or more oils/fats due to the Westernization of their diet.

Japanese traders and oil companies were significant players in the soy products trade from Manchuria. When Manchuria became the center of world soy production and export in the 1930s, the four Japanese trading and oil companies of Mitsui, Mitsubishi, Honen Oil, and Nisshin Oil handled over 80% of soy oil exports from Manchurian ports; Mitsui alone accounted for 45% and Mitsubishi for 25% (Table 2.4).

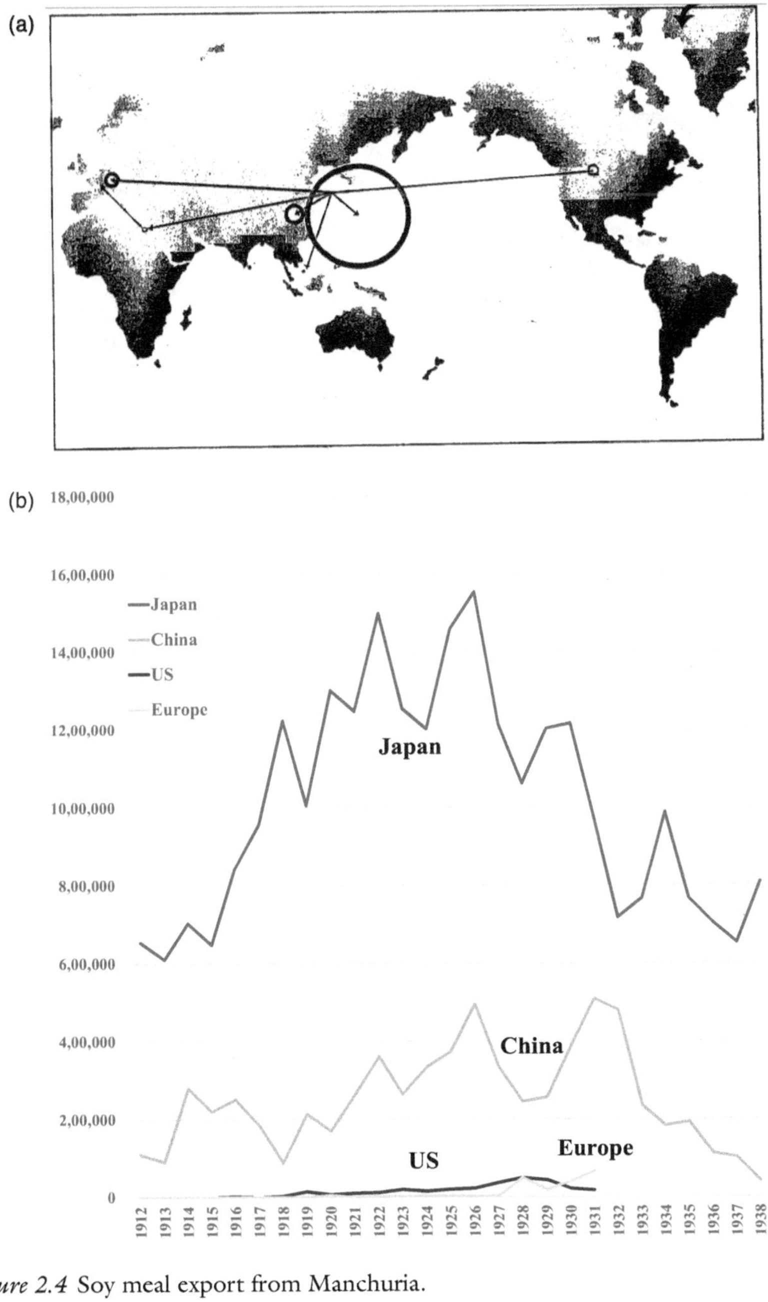

Figure 2.4 Soy meal export from Manchuria.

(a) Map illustrating exports in 1938; (b) Exports from Manchukuo from 1912 to 1938.

Source: Compiled by the author, based on data in Static Office of Manchukuo (1941, 102–107), courtesy of the Digital archives of the Institute for Economic and Business Research, Shiga University.

(a)

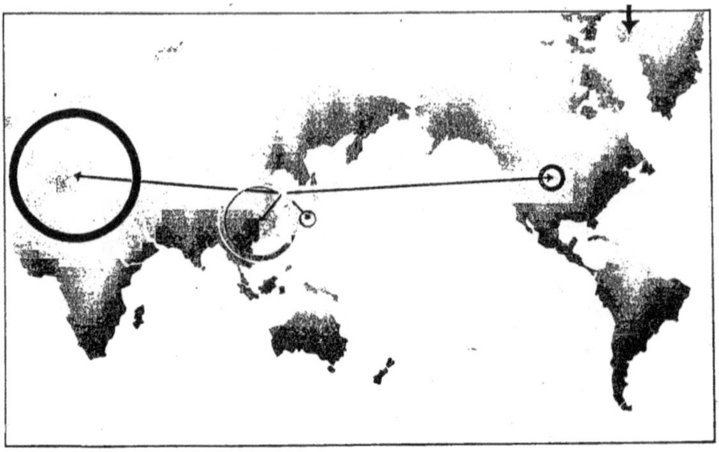

(b)

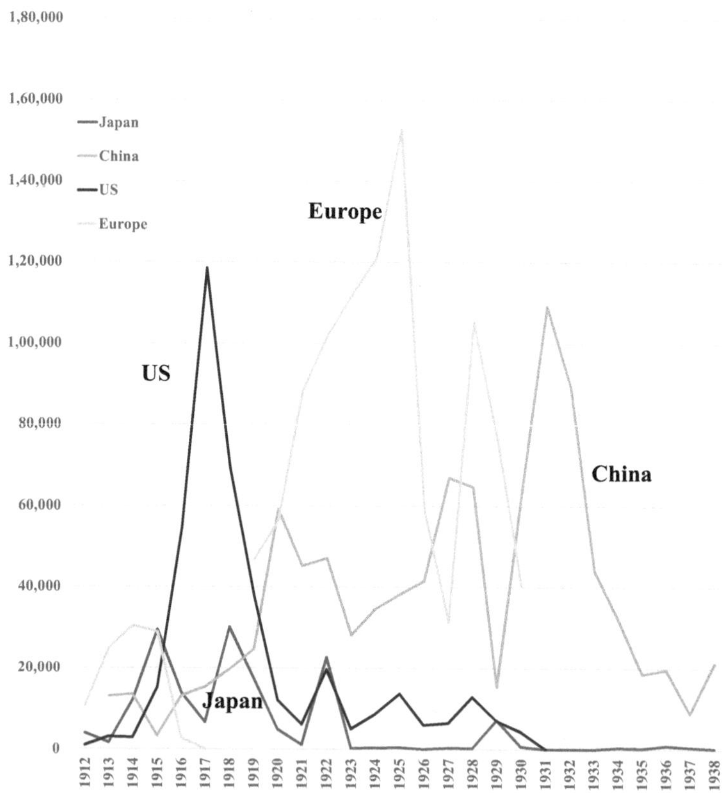

Figure 2.5 Soy oil export from Manchuria.

(a) Map illustrating exports in 1938; (b) Exports from Manchukuo from 1912 to 1938.

(a)

(b)

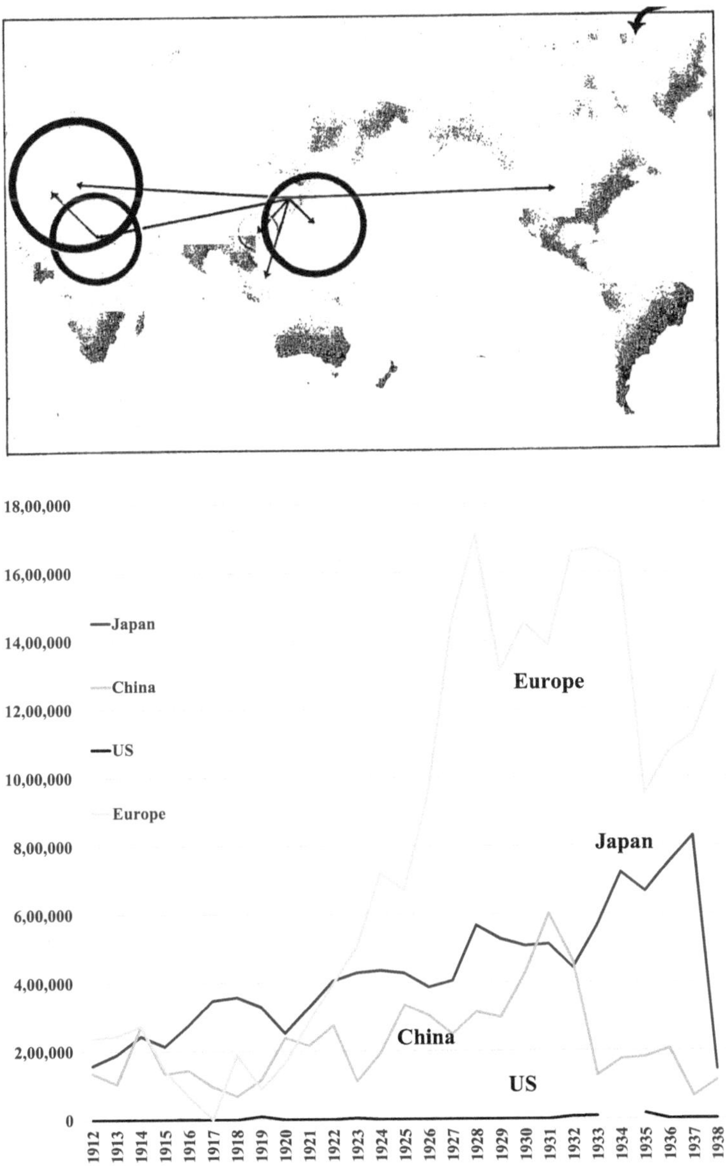

Figure 2.6 Soy bean export from Manchuria.

(a) Map illustrating exports in 1938; (b) Exports from Manchukuo from 1912 to 1938.

Table 2.4 Four Japanese companies exporting soy products from Manchuria in 1930 (unit: ton)

Company Name	*Destination*	*Soy bean*	*Soy meal*	*Soy oil*
Mitsui	Japan	37,947	234,512	17
	Korea	213	12,413	
	China	36,174	5,441	260
	South Sea	35,597	70	
	Europe	224,135	2,357	51,800
	US			2,687
	Total	334,066	254,793	54,764
	%	**17%**	**17%**	**45%**
Mitsubishi	Japan	29,464	260,775	
	Korea		927	
	China	570	938	394
	South Sea	13,062	36	
	Europe	100,083	14	27,148
	US		4,237	1,839
	USSR			614
	Total	143,179	266,927	29,995
	%	7%	**18%**	**25%**
Honen	Japan	162,200	30,630	4,027
	Korea		4,930	
	Europe		510	
	Total		36,070	
	%	**8%**	**2%**	**3%**
Nisshin	Japan	11,081	115,523	
	Korea		12	1
	China		28	18
	South Sea	4,484		
	Europe	19,396	2,763	9,489
	US	41	12,916	2,083
	Total	35,002	131,242	11,591
	%	**2%**	**9%**	**10%**
% of four Japanese companies		**34%**	**46%**	**83%**

Source: Compiled by the author based on data from SMR (1932, 95–96).

Note: Bold values are emphasis by the author.

These companies handled both processing and trade of soy products (bean, oil, and meal). At the same time, they made profits through speculative investments in financial trading over these commodities. According to a corporate history of Mitsubishi Corporation:

> We participated in soy bean trading, with soy beans as a financial commodity that we could buy from the market or sell to make a profit, or

> that we could crush in our own factories, and then sell soy oil and soy meal instead. In other words, soy-crushing worked as a kind of buffer in our profit-making strategy.
>
> (Mitsubishi Corporation 1986, 189)

When SUGIYAMA Kintaro, the president of Honen Oil, visited Manchuria, he commented that the main aim of the companies that owned the soy-crushing and oil-refining factories in Dalian "was to speculate on soy products, and the soy-crushing factories worked as a supplementary institution for such gambling" (Sugiyama 1957, 160). Nisshin Oil also admitted in their business reports that "our original business of soy-crushing became secondary, and the trading of Manchurian products became the main profit-making business in our operation" around 1933 and 1934 (Nisshin Oil Business Report for FY August 1933 to July 1934). In other words, speculation and profit-making were already the main aims of the soy companies and traders in the early stages of the development of Japan's soy-industry, long before the age of neoliberal globalization and the financialization of food and agriculture (Hiraga 2018).

Conflicts over Manchurian soy

As the international trade of soy products grew, local Manchurian forces also wanted a slice of the pie and began looking for ways to gain some of the incoming foreign currency from this successful "soy economy." Together with increasing Japanese military control in Manchuria, this contributed to the conflicts in this area that preceded WWII.

The development of the soy economy in Manchuria was not accomplished only by Japanese or foreign investors, of course. Although Japanese actors played significant roles in soy products' railway transportation using SMR, and in the export of these products from Manchurian ports, most soy bean production and most of the domestic trade in soy (from farms to the railway) was handled by local players in Manchuria. Local farmers and immigrant Chinese farmers cultivated soy, and local traders (糧桟) bought, stored, and transported it, as well as financing the farmers and selling daily goods to them (Zhu 2014). Japanese traders, including Mitsui&Co., tried to cut into this local trade; however, complicated local networks and multiple currencies prevented their entrance. So Japanese players mainly handled large-scale soy-crushing industries, railway transport, and international trade (Zhu 2014).

The soy-related industries and international trade were attractive sources of foreign currency for local warlords like ZHANG Zuolin of the Fengtian Clique, who needed foreign currency to buy arms from overseas. Eventually, in the 1920s, Zhang began operating soy-crushing factories and entered the local trade of soy products in Manchuria. His businesses began to push Japanese players out of the Manchurian soy business by building other railways parallel to SMR, supplying credit to farmers, and buying up soy (Zhu 2014; Yasutomi 2015, 104). Zhang was assassinated in 1928; the Manchurian Incident took place in 1931; and Japan's puppet state of Manchukuo was established in 1932. Although a comprehensive analysis of these conflicts and their consequences is beyond the scope of this book, the mounting tension between local forces and Japan over Manchurian soy has been suggested as one cause of the military conflicts between Japan and China/Manchuria (Kaneko 1991; Zhu 2014).

Soy gains American attention (1920s–1945)

The great success of Manchurian soy also caught the attention of the Americans. Although the United States is a major soy producer and exporter today, its soy production has a relatively short history, having begun in the 19th century, "as a curiosity until 1880," with about 2,000 acres planted in 1914. The domestic production of soy oil was too small to be recorded in official statistics until 1922, and its quality was too poor to be marketed (Eisenschiml 1929). American soy was cultivated mainly for seed and animal fodder until 1933 (Berlan, Bertrand, and Lebas 1977). As mentioned, before and during WWI, the United States imported soy oil from Manchuria, with the war leading to huge increases in these imports (Honen Oil 1944; USDA 1937). This led some cottonseed mills, especially on the west coast (i.e., facing Asia), to experiment with crushing imported soy bean during their off-season (Eisenschiml 1929). The use of soy meal for animal feed also raised interest among Americans. In 1929, the USDA sent the Oriental Agricultural Exploration Expedition to Asia to learn more about soy production (USDA 2009). The US government and the American Soybean Association (ASA), founded and organized in the 1920s, promoted the production of domestic soy and a soy-crushing industry in the United States, while placing protective duties to block the importation of soy bean and soy oil from Manchuria and tropical oils from Southeast Asia. When the country faced severe oil and fat shortages during WWII, the government and business interests actively campaigned to encourage people to save fats and oils for war needs (Prodöhl 2016) and demanded that oil products like margarine be made with "raw material produced on American soil" (Berlan et al. 1977). The domestic production and crushing of soy increased in the United States from the latter half of the 1930s, although not all American farmers were enthusiastic about soy cultivation. The actual motivation behind this increase in soy production requires other research, but the United States became the global leader in soy production, and Japan became the largest buyer of US soy, after WWII (as described in detail in later chapters).

Discussion

The modern big business of soy-crushing and the global trade of soy products began as a part of Japan's nation-building project, not to provide food for people but to accumulate capital and power.

Mass-produced soy oil and meal: Products and markets

Soy bean is harder and contains less oil than Japan's traditionally pressed oilseeds. The bean was used as food, but not for oil, for centuries in Japan. It was the modern capital-intensive machine-industry with powered crushing machines and solvent-extraction technologies that enabled mass-production of soy meal and soy oil. Based on historical records, I argue that Japanese *zaibatsu* and big oil companies played significant roles in this transformation. Nisshin Oil (co-founded by the Okura *zaibatsu*) built the biggest machine-powered oil-pressing factory in Dalian, Manchuria. The Japanese colonial institution of SMR and its corporate successor, Suzuki Shoten, introduced solvent-extraction, which was state-of-the-art technology at the time, in Manchuria and Japan. Their huge capital investment in the machinery and chemical-based processing methods enabled the mass-production of higher-quality soy meal (with less oil residue) that could be transported longer distances, as well as more efficient production of soy oil (by extracting more oil). In this way, soy became an industrial raw material, and soy products (meal, oil, and bean) became global commodities to be traded from Asia to the United States and European countries.

The mechanical mass-production factories required large-volume procurement of raw materials, which the big Japanese companies accomplished in Manchuria. Although the actual farming and local trade of soy were mainly handled by local people, Japanese businesses, including Nisshin Oil and Honen Oil, and the trading sectors of Mitsui and Mitsubishi, became the most significant traders of soy products from Manchuria. As a Japanese colonial agent, SMR also supported the development of the soy-industry in Manchuria through R&D, investing in transport and storage facilities and managing quality control and supply chains, all for the benefit of Japan.

Soy and the "visible hands" of business and government

Manchurian soy provided crucial business and political opportunities for the Japanese government and *zaibatsu* as they worked together to establish a modern state and expand to other parts of Asia. Japan began its modernization in the latter half of the 19th century as a latecomer to the capitalist world-economy. In order to avoid Western colonization and quickly develop as an independent modern nation-state, the Japanese government actively facilitated economic and political transformation. The government supported some of the existing rich families since the feudal era, like Mitsui and Sumitomo, and it also worked with the newly developed *zaibatsu*, like Mitsubishi, Okura, and Suzuki Shoten. The government gave them special support and orders to their traders to conduct the government's business, as well as to develop key industries and international trade to accumulate capital in Japanese hands.

It might be coincidental that the soy-crushing industry was taking off in Manchuria at the same moment that Japanese consulate offices, special banks, and government traders—the leading "trinity" of Japan's overseas expansion—were opening in key Manchurian cities. In any event, the situation was undeniably excellent for Japanese businesses that were closely linked with the government, including through colonial institutions like SMR. The soy-crushing industry and the export of soy products supported the growth of the Japanese companies and Japanese colonial institutions, thus indirectly supporting Japan's imperial expansion across Asia. The following chapters explore how Manchurian soy supported Japanese military actions in the coming decades.

The role of soy in food and capitalist history: The First Food Regime in the Asian context

The development of the soy-industry in and trade from Manchuria (soy meal to Japan, soy oil to the West, and soy bean to Japan and Europe) helped Japan accumulate capital for its state-building project. Soy meal fertilizer was used to modernize Japanese agriculture as purchased input to increase rice and mulberry leaf (hence silk) production. The increased production of rice was helpful to feed the Japanese people, especially factory workers and soldiers. But more important was the production of mulberry leaves to feed silkworms, so that Japan could increase its exports of raw silk and silk products and thus obtain foreign currency, that was crucial for supporting Japan's industrial revolution and economic development. Manchurian soy was not used directly to feed people; however, soy was incorporated into the processes of capital accumulation necessary for modernizing Japan. Therefore, I argue that the Japanese involvement in Manchurian soy was key to the First Food Regime in the Asian context (as also discussed in Hiraga and Hisano, 2017).

Soy oil made from Manchurian soy was exported to Europe and the United States from both Manchuria and Japan, leading to soy being recognized as an oilseed in the Western countries and becoming a global trade commodity. In this capacity, soy began its trajectory as one of the main crops behind large-scale forest eradication, from Manchuria in the 19th century to worldwide up to the present days (Yasutomi 2015, 102). In this chapter, I argue that soy production in Manchuria and the active involvement of modernizing Japan laid the foundation of the transformation and globalization of soy.

Bibliography

In English

Berlan, J., Bertrand, J., and Lebas, L. (1977) "The Growth of the American 'Soybean Complex' ", *European Review of Agricultural Economics*, 4(4), pp. 395–416.

Eisenschiml, O. (1929) "Domestic Soya Bean Oil", *Journal of the American Oil Chemists Society*, 6(4), pp.15–19.

Hiraga, M. (2018) "Financialization in Japanese agri-food regimes: Uncovering the role of sogo-shosha in global soy investment", in Bjorkhaug, H., Magnan, A., and Lawrence, G. (eds.), *The Financialization of Agri-Food Systems* (pp. 156–175). Routledge.

Hiraga, M. and Hisano, S. (2017) "The First Food Regime in Asian Context? Japan's Capitalist Development and the Making of Soybean as a Global Commodity in the 1890s-1930s", *AGST Working Paper Series* No. 2017-3, Asian Platform for Global Sustainability & Transcultural Studies (Japan Gateway Program), Kyoto University.

Prodöhl, I. (2016). "From Dinner to Dynamite : Fats and Oils in Wartime America". *Global Food History*, 2(1), pp. 31–50.

Prodöhl, I. (2023) *Globalizing the Soybean: Fat, Feed, and Sometimes Food, c. 1900–1950*, Routledge.

Shaw, N. (1911) *Soya Bean of Manchuria*, Statistical Dept. of the Inspectorate General of Customs.

USDA (1937) "Fats, Oils, and Oleaginous Raw Materials", Statistical Bulletin No. 59, May 1937.

USDA (2009) "Japan Agricultural Situation: The History of U.S. Soybean Exports to Japan 2009", *Foreign Agricultural Service GAIN Report*, available at: https://apps.fas.usda.gov/gainfiles/200901/146327093.pdf (accessed November 13, 2016).

In Japanese (with English translation by the author)

Hijikata, S. (1980) *Yokohama Specie Bank* (土方晋 [1980]『横浜正金銀行』（教育社歴史新書 日本史146）教育社).

Honen Oil (1944) *The Corporate History 20 Years* (豊年製油[1944] 『豊年製油株式會社二十年史』豊年製油).

Hori, K. (2009) *East Asia Capitalist History Theory 1* (堀和生 [2009] 『形成・構造・展開（東アジア資本主義史論 1）』 ミネルヴァ書房).

Ishii, K. ed. (2005) *Modern Japan Distribution History* (石井寛治 編 [2005] 『近代日本流通史』東京堂出版).

Ishii, K. (2012) *The Expansion Strategy of Imperial Japan* (石井寛治 [2012] 『帝国主義日本の対外戦略』名古屋大学出版会).

Japan Business History Institute. (1976) *A 100 Years of Mitsui Bussan* (日本経営史研究所 [1976] 『挑戦と創造: 三井物産100年のあゆみ』三井物産).

Kaneko, F. (1991) *A Study on Modern Japan's Investment in Manchuria* (金子文夫 [1991] 『近代日本における対満州投資の研究』近藤出版社).

Kasuga, Y. (2010) *Zaibatsu Traders and Imperial Japan* (春日豊 [2010] 『帝国日本と財閥商社: 恐慌・戦争下の三井物産』名古屋大学出版会).

Katsura, Y. (1976) "A Collapse of Zaibatsu: A Story of Suzuki Shoten", in Yasuoka (ed.), *Japan's Zaibatsu* (桂芳男「財閥化の挫折：鈴木商店」pp.178–223. 安岡重明 編 [1976]『日本の財閥』日本経済新聞社).

Kikuchi, K. (1994) *A History of Soybean Industry* (菊池一徳 [1994] 『大豆産業の歩み: その輝ける軌跡』光琳).

Kiyama, M. (2009) *Modern Japan and Mitsui Bussan* (木山実 [2009]『近代日本と三井物産: 総合商社の起源』日本史ライブラリー 21, ミネルヴァ書房).

Manshi-kai (Manchuria History Study Association 1964) *The Development of Manchuria: 40 Years* (満史会 [1964]『満州開発四十年史』下巻、満州開発四十年史刊行会).

Masuno, M. (1942) *Soybean and Its Industry in the World* (増野實 [1942]『世界の大豆と工業』河出書房).

Mishima, Y. (1979) *History of Mitsubishi Zaibatsu* (三島康雄 [1979]『三菱財閥史 明治編』教育社).

Mitsubishi Corporation (1986) *History of Mitsubishi Corporation ver.1* (三菱商事 [1986]『三菱商事社史 上』三菱商事株式会社).

Morikawa, H. (1978) *History of Japanese zaibatsu* (森川英正 [1978]『日本財閥史』（教育社歴史新書 日本史123） 教育社).

Nakajima, T. ed. (1967) *History of Industrial Development in Modern Japan: Food Industry* (中島常雄 編 [1967]『現代日本産業発達史 第18食品』現代日本産業発達史研究会).

Nisshin Oil (1969) *The Corporate History 60 Years* (日清製油株式会社 [1969] 『日清製油60年史』日清製油).

Oishi and Miyamoto eds. (1975) *Basic Knowledge on Japan's Capitalistic Development History* (大石嘉一郎、宮本憲一編集 [1975] 『日本資本主義発達史の基礎知識: 成立・発展・没落の軌跡』有斐閣).

Okura Zaibatsu Research Association (1982) *The Research on Okura Zaibatsu* (大倉財閥研究会 [1982]『大倉財閥の研究: 大倉と大陸』近藤出版社).

Ooura, M. and Hirano, S. eds. (1948) *Golden Flower: The History of Japan Oil Company* (大浦万吉・平野茂之 編 [1948]『黄金の花: 日本製油株式会社沿革史（改訂増補版）』新潮社).

Sakamoto, M. (2003) *Zaibatsu and Imperialism: Mitsui & Co. and China* (坂本雅子 [2003]『財閥と帝国主義: 三井物産と中国』ミネルヴァ書房).

Shibagaki, K (1968) *One Hundred Years of Mitsui and Mitsubishi* (柴垣和夫 [1968]『三井・三菱の百年: 日本資本主義と財閥』中央公論社).

SMR (South Manchuria Railway) (1924a) *On Soy Processing* (南満洲鉄道株式会社農務課 [1924]『大豆の加工』（産業資料 其21）満蒙文化協会).

SMR (South Manchuria Railway) (1924b) *On Oil-Press Industry in Manchuria* (南満洲鉄道庶務部調査課, [1924] 『滿洲に於ける油坊業』（滿鐵調査資料第23編）南滿洲鐵道株式會社庶務部調査課), also available at: https://dl.ndl.go.jp/pid/1877507

SMR (South Manchuria Railway) (1930) *The Trade Return Report from Southern Manchuria Ports* (南満州鉄道株式会社 [1930]『北支那貿易年報』南満州鉄道).

SMR (South Manchuria Railway) (1932) *The Development of Manchuria Economy* (滿鐵經濟調査會編 [1932] 『滿洲經濟の發達』南滿洲鐵道).

Static Office of Manchukuo (1941) *The Country Profile 1941* (満洲国国務院総務庁統計処、建国大学研究院図表班編纂 [1941] 満洲国国勢図表 康徳7年版), also available at: https://mokuroku.biwako.shiga-u.ac.jp/keywords/35971

Sugihara, K. (1996) *Formation and Structure of Inter-Asian Trade* (杉原薫 [1996]『アジア間貿易の形成と構造』（Minerva人文・社会科学叢書 4）ミネルヴァ書房).

Sugita, N. (1995) *The SMR Central Laboratory* (杉田望 [1995]『満鉄中央試験所』徳間書店).

Sugiyama, K. (1957) *My History (Kintaro Sugiyama)* (杉山金太郎 [1957]「杉山金太郎 私の履歴書」日本経済新聞社編『私の履歴書』（第4集）日本経済新聞社、pp.143–179).

Suzukishoten-museum (2014) *Suzuki Shoten Memorial Museum website* (鈴木商店記念館, available at: www.suzukishoten-museum.com (accessed April 7, 2024).

Ushiyama, K. (2008) "The Establishment of Japanese Capitalism: 1888 to World War 1", in Teruoka, S. (ed.), *Agriculture in the Modernization of Japan, 1850–2000* (pp. 53–98), Manohar Publishers & Distributors. (translation of 牛山敬二「第２章日本資本主義の確立：1880年代末から第１次世界大戦まで」pp. 29–69. 暉峻衆三 編 [2003] 『日本の農業150年: 1850〜2000年』有斐閣).

Usui, H. (2010) *Two "Oils" Will Change the World: The World Grain Market Enters a New Stage* (薄井寛 [2010] 『2つの「油」が世界を変える一新たなステージに突入した世界穀物市場』農山漁村文化協会).

Yasuoka, S. (1979) *Mitsui Zaibatsu (Early Modern to Meiji Era)* (安岡重明 [1979]『三井財閥史 近世・明治編』教育社).

Yasutomi, A. (2015) *The Stampede of Manchuria: The Hidden Structure* (安冨歩 [2015]『満洲暴走一隠された構造』角川書店).

Zhu, M. (2014) "Japanese Oil Companies Expansion to Manchuria from the Beginning of 20th Century to the End of WW2", Doctor thesis for Aichi Shukutoku University. (朱美栄「20世紀初頭から第2次世界大戦終結に至るまでの日系製油企業の満洲進出とその展開: 日清製油を中心に」学位論文（博士）愛知淑徳大学 2014年).

Websites

Business Archives Online (丸善企業史料統合データベース; for business reports of related companies) https://j-dac.jp/bao, Japan Digital Archives Center.

Kobe University Digital Archive Newspaper Clippings Collection (神戸大学附属図書館 デジタルアーカイブ) www.lib.kobe-u.ac.jp/sinbun/, Kobe University.

Kyoto University Rare Materials Digital Archive "Asia Depicted on Postcards" https://rmda.kulib.kyoto-u.ac.jp/en/collection/asia-pc, Kyoto University.
NDL Digital Collections (国立国会図書館デジタルコレクション) https://dl.ndl.go.jp/, National Diet Library (Japan).
Oil History Archive (東京油問屋市場「油歴史資料館」) www.abura.gr.jp, Tokyo Oil Wholesaler Market.
Shiga University Digital archives of the Institute for Economic and Business Research (滋賀大学経済経営研究所収集資料&デジタルアーカイブ検索システム) https://mokuroku.biwako.shiga-u.ac.jp, Shiga University.
Suzuki Shoten Memorial Museum (鈴木商店記念館) www.suzukishoten-museum.com, Suzukishoten-museum.

3 Expanding soy's versatility in multiple markets (the interwar period)

A colonial strategy and a means of business survival

Introduction

Once soy had become a capital-intensive mechanical-industry, the mass-production structure required continuous mass-sale of soy products. The Japanese soy-crushing companies, the origins of today's major edible oil suppliers, invested huge amounts of capital in large-scale soy-crushing factories. The special demand that arose during WWI provided them a timely opportunity to boost their development. After WWI ended, however, the companies faced an oversupply of their products. Soy oil, especially, had no market in Japan to begin with, and the fertilizer market was turning to chemical inputs over soy meal. The companies desperately needed to create markets for new soy products in order to survive, propelling a wave of research and development. The colonial institution of the South Manchuria Railway (SMR) also needed the soy-industry in Manchuria to support its mission as an agent of Imperial Japan. This chapter explores the efforts of SMR and these Japanese companies to develop versatile usages of soy and to expand soy's markets in non-food manufacturing and military supplies, as well as some food-processing, in the interval between the two world wars. These efforts were supported by advances in oleochemical technologies and protein engineering, and by the political economy of the 1930s, as Japan pursued further military conquests in Asia and the Pacific.

The relationship between capital investment and oil-extracting methods

Before exploring the development of various soy products, this section briefly outlines different oil-extracting methods, which produce different qualities of soy meal and oil, and their relationship with capital investment.

In general, animal fat is easy to use even for an individual—it just has to be cut from the meat. A few oil crops, like oil palm and olive, have soft-fleshed fruits that are relatively easy to squeeze for oil. It is more difficult to extract

DOI: 10.4324/9781032678733-4

oil from harder oilseeds. Some of the harder seeds, like sesame, perilla, and rapeseed, have such a high oil content that the oil can be extracted efficiently enough with simple, human-powered oil-pressing tools, and several of these have been used as oil sources since the premodern era. Soy, in contrast, contains much less oil (less than 20%) and the beans are hard, so it is natural that soy was traditionally considered a food rather than an oilseed in Japan and China.

In northeastern China, people had begun crushing soy some time before modernization (as discussed in Chapter 1). About 30 oil-pressing factories were reported in the Manchurian port city of Yingkou around the end of the 19th century. They used animals to pull millstones to crush the beans and manually operated wedge-presses to squeeze the oil out. This method was not very effective, and these mills produced low volumes of oil and still-oily meal, which, according to the report published by SMR, *On Soy Processing*, "could not meet the quality level necessary for export to the global market, so their market was limited to China" (SMR 1924a, 311). Figure 3.1 shows how soy meal and soy oil were transported around the 1930s in the northern China.

The British Swire Group is said to be the first to build a modern machine-driven oil-pressing factory in Yingkou, in 1896, which used steam power to operate presses with spiral steel-rollers. After the Russo-Japanese War (1904–1905), Japanese companies built more machine-press factories in Manchuria. KOTERA Sokichi (小寺壮吉) built such a factory in Yingkou, and Nisshin Oil built another, with the Okura *zaibatsu*'s support, in Dalian. Nisshin Oil's Dalian factory had the largest daily production capacity of 7,000 sheets of soy meal (about 200 tons), when local factories were producing about 100 or 200 sheets per day (SMR 1924a; Honen Oil 1944; Nisshin Oil 1969).

Before WWII, solvent-extraction methods were a cutting-edge technology. While the oil-pressing methods crushed soy to physically squeeze the oil out, solvent-extraction methods used chemical solvents (benzine or alcohol in those days) to extract the oil, efficiently producing high-quality soy meal containing little residual oil. However, building a factory that used solvents required a much larger capital investment. By 1924, the only factory using a solvent-extraction method in Manchuria was the Japanese Honen Oil's factory in Dalian, which was built by SMR's Central Laboratory and was expanded with the investment of Suzuki Shoten, the largest *zaibatsu* in those days (see Chapter 2 for details) (Honen Oil 1944, 2).

More efficient oil-extracting technologies were important to produce more soy oil, of course. But they were also important to produce higher-quality soy meal. To be useful as fertilizer, the meal should contain little oil residue, as oil hinders the growth of plants. Soy meal was the main product of the Japanese soy-crushing companies, as discussed in Chapter 2. Table 3.1

(a)

(b)

Figure 3.1 Shipping soy meal (a) and soy oil (b) at Tsingtao Small Island port in 1939. (Photograph courtesy of the North China Railway Archive [The North China Railway Archive Committee], (a) photo number 3705-026739-0; (b) photo number 3705-026737-0, available at https://codh.rois.ac.jp/north-china-railway/).

Table 3.1 Differences in soy meal quality according to the different oil-extraction methods

Shape of soy meal	*Oil press/extract methods*	*% of oil yield*	*% of meal yield*	*% of oil residue in soy meal*	*% of oil protein in soy meal*
Round meal	Pressure (600–700 pound)	About 10	About 86	8	40
Square meal	Pressure (1700–2000 pound)	About 12	About 84	5	43
Flake meal	Extract with benzine	About 15	About 80	1	45

Source: Compiled by the author based on data from Masuno (1942, 159).

shows the different amounts of oil content remaining in soy meal according to the different oil-extracting methods, based on a study conducted in the 1940s. In those days, soy meal produced by different methods took different shapes and forms. An old-fashioned oil press powered by humans or animals produced soy meal pressed into round sheets, so people called it "round meal." The machine-powered oil presses produced square sheets, so people called it "square meal." The solvent-extraction method produced not sheets but flakes because the meal was not pressed physically, and hence it was known as "scattered" or "flaked meal" (this book calls it "flake meal").

In this way, although soy-crushing had begun in Manchuria before the British or Japanese came at the end of the 19th century, it was these foreign capital that developed soy-crushing into a mechanical-industry that could mass-produce soy meal and soy oil to meet the volume and quality required for global trade.

The South Manchuria Railway's R&D for the soy-industry

The SMR was a semiofficial "national policy corporation" and its Central Laboratory functioned as a Japanese colonial institution with the mission of researching and developing the industrial possibilities of agricultural products in Manchuria. The development of the Manchurian soy-industry and soy trade was important to support SMR's colonial operations, and thus Japan's empire-building. Its soy-related R&D included oil-extraction technology with benzine, which was used by Suzuki Shoten (later Honen Oil); oil-extraction technology with alcohol, which was used by the Manchuria Soy-Industry Company (満洲大豆工業); and hydrogenation of soy oil (solidifying liquid soy oil into hardened oil), which was used by the Dairen Oil Industry Corporation (大連油脂工業), among many others.

The hydrogenation of liquid vegetable oil to make solid fats, better known today as trans fats, was important in those days because large amounts of hardened oil were demanded as industrial raw materials. The SMR Central Laboratory is said to have been the first to industrialize the hydrogenation of soy oil in Manchuria, in 1916. SMR established the Dairen Oil Industry Corporation to manufacture hydrogenated soy oil, using nickel as the catalyst to allow hydrogen gas to be added to the fat. The company had the capacity to annually produce 7,200 tons of industrial material for manufacturing soap and candles, and 1,100 tons of edible material for manufacturing shortening, artificial tallow, and lard. As part of its oil- and fats-related research, the SMR Central Laboratory also developed high-quality alcohol and "artificial petrol" out of soy oil (Masuno 1942, 168–169).

Soy protein, which is another name for soy meal, was also important as an industrial material at the time. Before the use of petrochemicals became widespread, plant- and animal-based raw materials were commonly used for industrial purposes. Protein engineering was developing rapidly in the West, and SMR researchers learned from the Western innovations. The SMR Central Laboratory researched technology to manufacture paint and plastic out of soy protein. For example, one of the Laboratory's researchers, SUZUKI Tsuneo (also known as Yasuo, 鈴木庸生), registered a water-based paint made out of soy protein, named "Solight," in 1913, and another, SATO Sadakichi (佐藤定吉), succeeded in manufacturing plastic out of soy protein, naming it "Sato-light," in 1915 (SMR 1924a, 516–524).

Manchurian soy became more and more important as an industrial raw material in the 1930s and 1940s, as Japan continued to militarize and expand its colonization of Asia and the Pacific. Japanese researchers focused on the vegetable and fish oil resources available in Japan's occupied territories in Asia. In this context, the SMR Central Laboratory in Manchuria was a significant player in Japan's empire-building.

The corporate efforts to create new markets for soy meal

The market for soy meal, which had once been Japanese soy-crushing companies' main product, shrank drastically after WWI, because Japan's heavy chemical industry had developed enough to supply cheaper ammonium sulfate for fertilizer. In addition, the prices of rice and silk fell in the post-war recession, significantly reducing the ability of Japanese rice and silk farmers (who must grow the mulberry leaves that silkworms eat) to purchase fertilizer (Sakaguchi 2003). The business reports of soy-crushing companies in the latter half of the 1920s repeatedly discuss the shrunken soy meal market because of the decreased demand for fertilizer. For example, in 1928, Nisshin Oil reported that

> Japanese farmers, the main consumers of our soy meal business, have been suffering from the continuous depression of prices, so they are reducing the amount of fertilizer they purchase, or choosing cheaper chemical fertilizers, thus reducing demand for soy meal.
>
> (Nisshin Oil Business Report for FY August 1928 to July 1929)

The fertilizer market was the company's "lifeline," said Honen Oil, the main beneficiary of SMR Central Laboratory's benzine oil-extraction technology (Honen Oil 1944, 45). However, the flake meal Honen Oil produced with the solvent-extraction method was a new and unfamiliar product in those days, and Japanese farmers preferred their accustomed pressed soy meal (either manually pressed round sheets or machine-pressed square sheets). Thus, Honen Oil trained its attention on selling, developing new marketing methods that it applied to all of its products, not just meal. For instance, they began branding and promoting specific soy products for different purposes and established their own retail networks to sell these products. Honen Oil's brand names included "Yutaka Mame" (rich bean) for the fertilizer market and "Sakura Mame" for the raw material of miso and soy-sauce manufacturing. The company also approached government-affiliated institutions like agricultural experiment stations and fertilizer testing stations, agricultural committees in each of the Japanese prefectures, and respected farmers in each area to promote Honen Oil's flake meal. In addition, the company utilized the available media of the day, publishing posters and leaflets, as well as advertisements in newspapers and magazines. They even organized lotteries, prizes, and gifts for their customers (Honen Oil 1944, 78–82).

The corporate effort to sell soy protein as an edible material

The Japanese term meaning "soy meal" is *mame kasu*, and *kasu* can have the connotation of "leftovers" or "dregs"—not very attractive for product names. Due to corporate efforts, the general name for soy meal was gradually changed to a term that translates as "soy protein." Today, it is often called "defatted soy," especially when it is used as a food ingredient.

In fact, although soy protein (or defatted soy) is a very common ingredient in many kinds of processed food today, it was difficult to persuade Japanese food processors to accept it as an edible ingredient at first. The president of Honen Oil related an episode that illustrates the difficulty the company faced. Honen Oil asked a government fermentation testing station to test their soy meal, and they obtained evidence that soy meal could be used just as whole soy beans were to make soy sauce. Still, Kikkoman, the major soy sauce company, was reluctant to use soy meal as an ingredient, because they feared it would damage the company's image if consumers found out that

Kikkoman was using *kasu* (leftovers or dregs) to make their soy sauce. In the end, they agreed to use soy meal only for making the starter for their soy sauce production. Even for that, Kikkoman asked Honen Oil to erase the words *mame kasu* (soy meal) from their packages when they delivered to Kikkoman's factories (Sugiyama 1957, 170–171).

Despite these corporate efforts, it took a natural disaster to popularize soy meal as an edible product among Japanese people. When the Great Kanto Earthquake struck the Tokyo area in 1923, the city needed emergency food, and soy meal was provided to feed people in the disaster area. According to a memoir of the Nisshin Oil company, "This made people acknowledge to some degree that soy meal was food" (Nisshin Oil 1969, 81).

As these episodes suggest, soy meal did not just naturally become part of the Japanese diet. Instead, it took active corporate efforts to persuade people to accept soy meal as a food ingredient—even in Japan, where people had eaten soy foods for centuries. This history of the soy-industry also indicates that its development was neither initiated by consumer demand nor an intentional step toward national food security.

Around the same time, the potential of using soy meal for manufacturing monosodium glutamate (MSG) was investigated. Ajinomoto[1] had been using wheat as MSG's main ingredient, but their laboratory research found that soy protein could be used to manufacture MSG at a commercial production level. Based on their innovation and trial production in the 1920s and 1930s, Ajinomoto built their own soy-crushing company as a subsidiary in 1933 (宝製油株式会社) and began using their own soy meal to manufacture MSG (Ajinomoto 1971, 291, 307–311). Ajinomoto and Honen Oil eventually consolidated into J-Oil Mills, which sells its edible oil products under the brand name of Ajinomoto today.

The corporate effort to develop the soy protein industry

While a corporate effort was needed to sell soy meal as a food ingredient, soy's use in non-food products was also being explored vigorously. For Japan, which lacks petroleum resources and had little animal production in those days, soy protein became important as a raw material for making many industrial materials such as glues and plastics. Japanese companies, as well as SMR and the military, were very interested in R&D with soy meal.

Soy casein, for example, was one of the new products that drew a great deal of attention. In those days, milk casein, made of milk protein, was used to manufacture glue (as a kind of agglutinative agent). However, this was before Japan began full-scale livestock development, so its production of milk casein was very limited, with only 50 to 60 tons produced annually in the 1940s. Therefore, Japan imported about 5,000 to 6,000 tons of milk casein annually from Australia and Argentina. Such bio-based casein was an important industrial material before the age of petrochemicals being used to manufacture glue, paint, plywood, and artificial fiber, as well as military supplies.

Honen Oil needed to create more soy meal markets, and the company realized that industrial and military demand was increasing, so they strengthened their soy protein R&D. The company began producing their patented soy glue as "Honen glue" in 1933 (Honen Oil 1944, 117–119; 1963, 48–49) .

Another major oleochemical company, Nippon Oil & Fats (日本油脂), also succeeded in producing soy casein, and rapidly increased the scale of their production under military protection and with military promotion (NOF 1967, 344–345). By the 1940s, when Japan was fighting the Pacific War, several other companies produced soy casein, which was used in the manufacture of automobiles, airplanes, and military products. Thus, the Japanese government, military, and big business worked together to improve the quality of soy casein and rapidly increase its production (Masuno 1942, 198–199). Soy casein was also used as a pesticide adjuvant, so the Ministry of Agriculture and Forestry of Japan also promoted using soy to manufacture agricultural spreading agents (NOF 1967, 347), while the production of a soy-protein-based artificial fiber to replace wool reached the commercial level by the end of the 1930s. A newspaper article at the time praised soy meal as the most important source of protein for Japanese manufacturing industries (Taiwan Daily News 1938).

The importance of soy meal for military projects

The business necessity to expand the markets for soy meal became a national and military project as Japan continued to mobilize for war. The progress of the soy-industry was supported by concurrent scientific and technological development in the protein industries, and by the increasing importance of soy protein as a military material to substitute for petrol. In 1940, an industry association of soy protein manufacturers was established (日本大豆蛋白質製品組合). The industry continued R&D of soy casein, soy glue, soy plastic, soy fiber, and other soy protein products, with the support of Japan's Ministry of Commerce and Industry. An expert on the soy-industry at the time, MASUNO Minoru, recommended that the industry should aim to develop soy protein products as its main business, while also improving the quality of soy oil (Masuno 1942, 205), indicating that soy meal for industrial and military usage was the more important part of the business in those days.

The corporate effort to promote soy oil as an edible oil

Soy meal and soy oil are twin products: the modern soy-industry that mass-produced soy meal also mass-produced soy oil, and thus they also needed to find sufficient markets for the oil. Because there was very little demand for soy oil in Japan, Japanese soy-crushing companies first exported the oil to Western countries. However, the drastic increase of soy oil imports from the Far East during WWI led Western countries to encourage their own soy-crushing industries. As we saw in Chapter 2, European countries began importing more soy beans (a raw material) to process themselves and reduced their imports of soy oil (a product) from the latter half of the 1920s to the 1930s. This move shrank the soy oil export market for Japanese companies; now, the Japanese soy companies needed to create a new market to sell their soy oil domestically.

Expanding the Japanese market for vegetable oil: The precedent case of rapeseed oil

Traditionally, Japanese people pressed vegetable oils from perilla, rapeseed, or cottonseed, mainly for lighting oil (as discussed in Chapter 1). Before modernization began, the production of rapeseed oil with water-powered tools had reached commercial levels, supporting domestic trade from Western Japan to the capital of Edo (today's Tokyo). The need for vegetable oils for lighting, however, drastically shrank with modernization, because of the introduction of gas lamps and electricity. Significant amounts of fossil fuels were already being imported by the end of the 19th century (Tokyo Oil Wholesaler Market 2000; Nakajima ed. 1967, 493).

Luckily, rapeseed oil has high lubricity. A method of mixing ash into oil to refine it (*shirashime-yu*) had been developed, and this refined rapeseed oil was found to be suitable for lubricating machinery and for hardening (quenching) steel (Tsujimoto 1916, 331). Japan's industrial development and military expansion rapidly increased the use of steel and machinery, in turn increasing the demand for lubricating oil and quenching oil, especially after the Sino-Japanese War (Tokyo Oil Wholesaler Market 2000). Rapeseed oil was used for lighting fuel on trains too. So the military and the government offices like the Railway Bureau became large buyers of rapeseed oil in modernizing Japan (Ooura and Hirano eds. 1948, 26). As Japan fought in the Sino-Japanese War and the following battles with Russia and China, the Japanese army, navy, arsenals, and railway bureaus gave huge orders for rapeseed oil, which saved rapeseed traders, according to Yoshihara Shoten, a major oil trader that mainly dealt in rapeseed oil in those days (Hirano 1973, 33). In this way, rapeseed oil was able to find a new market.

The corporate effort to create markets for soy oil

Soy oil had no market in Japan to begin with. Honen Oil "really needed to make painstaking efforts to make soy oil popular among Japanese," recalled its corporate history (Honen Oil 1944, 48). Cheaper soy oil was sometimes mixed into more expensive sesame oil or rapeseed oil to add volume, but it was difficult to attract customers for soy oil itself.

In order to create a new market for soy oil, Japanese soy-crushing companies turned their efforts to refining it to make it edible. With this goal, Honen Oil learned an advanced oil-refining technology from the rapeseed oil industry, invited PhD-holding engineers to work with the company, and invested in new machinery. It began selling its "Refined Soy Oil" (Soy *Shirashimeyu*, 大豆白絞油) in the Japanese food market in 1923 (Honen Oil 1944, 48–50). Having no previous connection with the food industry, Honen Oil had to establish sales channels from scratch. According to the corporate history, even after its edible soy oil products went to market, "there was very little interest in soy oil among Japanese consumers, and we really needed to conduct more research and promotion for soy oil" (Honen Oil 1944, 95).

Nisshin Oil purchased new refining machines, invited an expert from Germany, invested 127,000 yen to build a new factory (Nisshin Oil 1969, 83–84), and, in 1924, launched sales of its first edible soy oil product: Nisshin Salad Oil. This remains the company's major product to this day. Like Honen Oil, Nisshin Oil had no connection with the food industry and hence needed to create a completely new sales channel. In order to promote its soy oil products in the Japanese food market, the company tried to introduce soy oil to the dormitories of the Imperial Household Agency, or to the home economics classes at a women's college. The company also held events to demonstrate how to make tempura, organized special sales with cash vouchers, and published newspaper advertisements for their products (Nisshin Oil 1969, 306–310).

It was the time that the marketing of new products via newspapers, magazines, and posters first became popular. Japanese vegetable oil companies took advantage of these media to promote not just their products but soy oil and vegetable oil in general. They needed to increase the habit of eating more oil and fat among Japanese people before they could sell their edible oil products. Despite such corporate efforts, the average daily consumption of edible oil remained less than 3 g before WWII, and "it was only after WWII that soy oil was fully disseminated and became a daily foodstuff for Japanese people" (Honen Oil 1963, 31, 34).

The development of hardened oil and the oleochemical industries

Oleochemistry, the study of plant-, animal-, and marine-based oils and fats, developed rapidly in the West around the end of the 19th century and the beginning of the 20th century. As the science and technologies developed, it became easier to substitute oils/fats of different origins for each other. The technology of hardening liquid oil into hydrogenated fat that stays solid at room temperatures was also developed around that time, and hardened oils became important raw materials in the manufacturing of a wide variety of products. The range of industrial uses for oil/fat products also continued to expand. Concurrently, soy- and oil-related companies transformed from businesses based on craftwork and manual manufacturing into capital- and resource-intensive businesses. A Japanese industry association described this shift: "the industry used to employ manual workers who had craftsmanship, like soap-making craftsmen, but now it became a world-level oleochemical industry with university graduates in advanced science" (JOPA 1972, 41). Some of these university-educated technical experts began to lead the industry as the executive managers of key companies. This section focuses on how soy produced in Manchuria and fish taken from the seas around the Korean Peninsula became important raw materials of these oil-related industries, and how the production of hardened oil was developed especially for the military supply industries as Japan entered the wars of the 1930s–1940s.

The production of hardened or hydrogenated oil (now better known as trans fats) in Japan was also initially geared to export to Europe, especially to take advantage of the rapid increase of demand during WWI. The British company Lever Brothers was the first to begin producing hardened oil in Japan. Lever Brothers chose Amagasaki (near Osaka) as their foothold for the expansion of their business in East Asia. They built a large-scale factory that could process oil crops and manufacture soap, glycerin, hardened oil, and other oleochemical products. The factory began supplying hardened oil in 1913 (JOPA 1972, 43). Around the same time, Japanese university-educated engineers at a government laboratory in the Ministry of Agriculture and Industry developed original methods of producing hydrogenated oil and established a company in 1914 to produce hardened oils.

These two pioneering companies, however, failed in later years. Thus, the company that actually laid the foundation for today's Japanese hardened oil industry was Suzuki Shoten, the largest *zaibatsu* of the time, whose oil section (which later became Honen Oil) was the leader in the soy oil industry. Along with its processing of Manchurian soy, Suzuki Shoten exported fish oil to Europe, first as liquid oil, and then, after 1915–1916, as hardened oil. The company conducted research on the manufacturing of hardened oil at its Hyogo factory and also built a few more factories for this project. Some records indicate that Suzuki Shoten invested more than half a million yen, huge investment at the time, in its hardened oil project. Later, it bought up various other pioneering projects in hardened oil in Japan, becoming the leading company in this field, which later became Nippon Oil & Fats (linked to today's NOF Corporation).

Table 3.2 Uses of hardened oils in Japan in 1936

	Volume (ton)	%
Laundry soap	45,000	37.7%
Face/body soap	10,000	8.4%
Vet for spinning	3,000	2.5%
For making candle	12,000	10.0%
Edible oil/fat	**4,800**	**4.0%**
For making oleic acid, stearin	2,500	2.1%
For export	39,350	32.9%
Glycerin from decomposed fatty acid	2,800	2.3%
Total	119,450	100.0%

Source: Compiled and the percent calculated by the author based on data from Kubota (1937, 372–379).

Note: Bold letter and value are emphasis by the author.

The technology for hardening oils is the same for making margarine or shortening. The main aim of the newly emerged Japanese hardened oil manufacturers, however, was to supply non-food industrial raw materials. As an industry expert said, "hardened oil was a matter of soap and glycerin for Japan" (Kubota 1929); only 4% of the hardened oil produced in 1936 was destined for edible products, while more than 40% was used to make soap, and more than 30% was exported (Table 3.2).

It was only after WWII that hardened oil was produced more for edible purposes in Japan; by 1955, edibles accounted for over 20% of the hardened oil production (NOF 1967, 455–457). When margarine became popular among Japanese people in the post-WWII era, the industry was dominated by a few large companies that had established their businesses on non-food products during the war.

Military motivations to expand the hardened oil market

Similar to the soy oil industry, the Japanese hardened oil industry owed its initial development to special orders from European countries during WWI, so it also faced the loss of the export market after the war ended. The Japanese companies that had overexpanded their production capacity for hardened oil also needed to create a new domestic market after WWI. In that corporate effort, a conflict occurred between the Japanese oil companies that manufactured hardened oil from Manchurian soy and from fish from the seas around the Korean Peninsula, and the Japanese soap companies that mainly used imported beef tallow and coconut oil to manufacture soap.

According to the Kao Soap company (today's Kao Corporation), the modern soap industry in Japan was established using imported beef tallow and coconut oil as their main raw materials. The soap industry persuaded the Japanese government to repeal a tariff on beef tallow to reduce the cost of raw materials and to encourage soap and glycerin production. The Japanese companies that manufactured hardened oil, led by Suzuki Shoten and Asahi Denka (linked to today's ADEKA), opposed this action. They emphasized the importance of producing glycerin from raw materials that could be sourced from the territories under Japanese control. The oil companies also submitted reports to the Navy Explosive Factory in Kanagawa in which they claimed that the quality of glycerin made from hardened oil and from beef tallow was the same (Kao Soap 1940, 578). The soap companies objected, arguing that the domestically produced hardened oil was inferior to imported beef tallow in quality, volume, and price. In the end, the Japanese Navy changed their policy to approve hardened oil in addition to beef tallow as raw materials for manufacturing glycerin in 1924. The Japanese government also agreed to readjust the import tariff on beef tallow in 1926 (Kao Soap 1940, 585). As this episode demonstrates, the oil companies used a discourse of national security to expand their market. They emphasized the importance of Japan being self-sufficient in glycerin for military purposes, and they even requested that the government protect the Japanese domestic oleochemical industries and the oil resources available in Asia.

As Figure 3.2 shows, domestic glycerin production increased rapidly from the middle of the 1920s, while the import of glycerin stagnated. With Japan's military escalation, the importance of the Japanese oil-related companies became a national security issue rather than purely a matter of business.

The concentration of oleochemical industries with zaibatsu *capital*

As they competed over the domestic glycerin market, the Japanese oil companies that had processed soy or fish began making soap, and the Japanese soap companies began making hardened oil. As a result, various oil-related businesses, including soy-crushing, oil-pressing, fish oil-processing, soap-manufacturing, and hardened-oil-manufacturing, merged into a more consolidated oleochemical and petrochemical industry. Advances in oleochemical science and technologies supported this development by making it easier to switch among the different oil/fat resources and their wide range of products. In a competitive market, through mergers and acquisitions, an oligopoly emerged, with a few dominant large companies. In the hardened oil industry, three companies, Nippon Oil & Fats (日本油脂), Asahi Denka

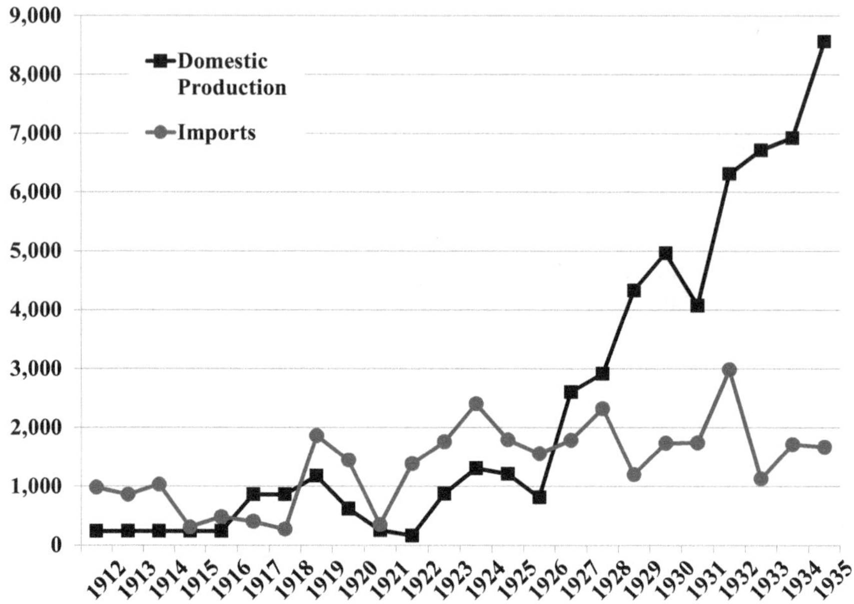

Figure 3.2 Imports and domestic production of glycerin in Japan, 1912–1935 (unit: ton).

Source: Produced by the author based on data from NOF (1967, 59).

(旭電化), and Oxyhydrogen Oil (酸水素油脂), collaborated to dominate most of the market (Ueno 1953), while the soap companies came together to form a national industry association in 1925 (全国石鹸製造業連合会) (Kao Soap 1940, 632).

As the industry consolidated, it attracted larger capital investment. While some of the established *zaibatsu* remained powerful, some new *zaibatsu* also emerged and became active in investing more in the new arenas of the chemical and military industries. "It was like a storm of mergers and acquisitions by monopoly capital taking over the industries," as one commentator described the situation in the latter half of the 1930s (Kao Soap 1940, 637). In addition to Suzuki Shoten, the Okawa *zaibatsu*, the Furukawa *zaibatsu*, and the Nisso *Konzern* invested in the hardened oil companies (NOF 1967, 158). Nippon Chisso and Nippon Sangyo, groups that had dealt in fish oil from the seas around Korea, actively invested in the oil-processing industry and developed their oleochemical business based on fish oil. Japan had annexed the Korean peninsula in 1910, and the colonial government advised Mitsui to consolidate the Korean oil and fertilizer business (Kao

Soap 1940, 678; NOF 1967, 159). The Nippon Sangyo group (Nissan *Konzern*) emerged under the leadership of AIKAWA Yoshisuke (also known as AYUKAWA, 鮎川義介). The group expanded its fishery business into the fish oil-based oleochemical industry, merging with several other companies, including the remains of Lever Brothers' Amagasaki factory and hardened oil factories related to Suzuki Shoten. These companies were consolidated into Nippon Oil & Fats Co. (日本油脂株式会社) in 1937, which became the leading oleochemical company in Japan.

The newer "emerging zaibatsu*"*

As Japan went deeper into war, especially after the Manchurian Incident in 1931, the Japanese government increased the military budget and promoted military-related industries. Some capitalists, middle-sized companies, and scientific research institutions entered the military-related industrial sectors to gain budgetary support. They rapidly developed into the "emerging *zaibatsu*"(新興財閥), including Nissan, Nisso, Mori, Nitchitsu, and Riken. The corporate groups in hierarchy structures, including old and new zaibatsu in the 1930s and 1940s, are sometimes labeled as *Konzern* ("concerns"), following the German cases. While the older *zaibatsu* like Mitsui and Mitsubishi dominated the heavy industries, these "emerging *zaibatsu*" more actively invested in the newer industrial sectors of military supply and electrochemical industries, and they rapidly developed by receiving profitable military orders under the protection and promotion of the government and the military (Tamaki 1976, 371–373). The oil- and fat-related industries, including the manufacturing of hardened oil and glycerin, had become an attractive sector for such emerging *zaibatsu*. The Nissan *Konzern* included Nippon Oil & Fats, which produced hardened oil, and Nippon Suisan, which processed seafood. They developed groups of companies that manufactured hardened oil, glycerin, soap, fish oil, and seafood based on resources from Manchuria and Korea.

The older zaibatsu*: Dominating trade in the Japanese food industries*

The older *zaibatsu* traders remained active in the trading sectors of oilseeds and oil-related products. In addition to Mitsui&Co., which led the international trade of Manchurian soy bean and soy products, Mitsubishi Corporation, the trading sector of the Mitsubishi *zaibatsu*, began full-scale trading of soy products in 1919. Mitsubishi established their Oil and Fat Section in Kobe in 1920, bought up the factory of Dalian Oil and the Fat Industry Corporation (大連油脂工業会社) in 1921, and utilized these assets to trade Manchurian soy products (bean, oil, and meal) to Japan and the world. The international trade of Manchurian soy products remained one of the main profit-makers among Mitsubishi Corporation's oil/fat and fertilizer sectors (Mitsubishi Corporation 1986, 188–189).

Some *zaibatsu* groups, including Mitsui and Mitsubishi, also became strong players in the modern food system of Japan, especially in supplying basic ingredients like wheat flour, sugar, and edible oils. While the recession in the 1920s drove Suzuki Shoten into bankruptcy, it also "provided a wonderful arena for *zaibatsu* capital to expand, as they had established the *Konzerns* by then" (Shibagaki 1968, 7). The hard times for many people and smaller businesses offered opportunities for bigger capital to buy up companies and dominate the markets. Oil-related and food businesses became embedded in these complexes.

A great deal of research is published in Japanese on the *zaibatsu* and *sogo-shosha*. Most of the previous *zaibatsu* literature focuses on their influence in the fields of finance or heavy industry, with much less attention to food or bio-based oils. However, the influence of *zaibatsu* in the Japanese food system was significant, especially in the early modernization period. SASAMA Yoshifumi, who compiled a history of the Japanese food industry up to the 1960s, argued that domination of the Japanese food industries by the *zaibatsu*-led oligopoly was established by the end of WWI, especially in the primary processing industries such as flour-milling, oil-refining, and sugar-manufacturing (Sasama 1979, 377). By the 1930s, two companies, Nisshin Seifun (of Mitsubishi) and Nipon Seifun (of Mitsui), controlled about 80% of flour-milling in Japan. Japanese sugar production in those days was based on sugar from occupied Taiwan, and the government traders were deeply involved there, thus Taiwan Seito (of Mitsui), Meiji Seito (of Mitsubishi), and Dainippon Seito (of the Fujiyama *Konzern*) dominated the sugar markets (Nakajima ed. 1967; Sasama 1979). Another study on *zaibatsu* calculated their part in the food industries around 1937, as shown in Table 3.3. Soy and oil industries are overlooked in this previous *zaibatsu* research, but they were dominated by Suzuki Shoten and the Okura *zaibatsu*, as this book demonstrates.

Soy's transformation into a military raw material

Before petrochemical industries flourished, animal-, fish-, and plant-based oils were important raw materials for industry and military sectors, especially during and after WWI. As more machines, such as combat vehicles, tanks, and airplanes, were used to wage war, more oil and fat were needed to keep them running smoothly, and the vegetable oil industry developed by collaborating with the government to pursue its modern wars.

MURAYAMA Takeshi, who researched the global situation of the oil-related industries in the 1930s, commented that bio-based oil and fat in those days

Table 3.3 Major Japanese flour mills and sugar manufacturers and their related *zaibatsu*, around 1937

Flour mills	Nisshin 日清製粉	Nippon 日本製粉	Nitto 日東製粉
Daily production capacity (barrel)?	26,500	20,800	5,000
Its % in domestic market	about 38%	about 30%	about 7%
Zaibatsu group	**Mitsubishi**	**Mitsui**	**Mitsubishi**
Sugar manufacturers	Taiwan 台湾製糖	Meiji 明治製糖	Dainippon 大日本製糖
Its % in domestic market	27.8%	20.2%	26.4%
Zaibatsu group	**Mitsui**	**Mitsubishi**	**Fujiyama**

Source: Compiled by the author based on data from Takahashi and Aoyama (1938, 250–253).

Note: Bold letters are emphasis by the author.

> had important roles, as they were essential military supplies that were required to wage wars, because glycerin made of various ingredients was a raw material for explosives, as was castor oil for aviation oil, rapeseed oil as lubricant for ship engines, and rapeseed and whale oil as quenching oil to harden steel, among others.
>
> (Murayama 1941, 1)

Modern warfare required huge amounts of steel and machinery as well as explosives; hence, the demand for oil and oil crops surged as crucial resources for the manufacturing of glycerin, lubricant, glue, casein, substitutes for other oils and for rubber, and many other products. As the producers of such military supplies, the oil producers and oleochemical companies gained new importance for governments preparing to wage war.

The Japanese oil-related industries collaborated with the military-government (although the extent to which they did so willingly or were forced to do so is uncertain). Honen Oil, for example, built their own research institute, Sugiyama Industrial Chemistry Laboratory (杉山産業化学研究所), where they conducted research on soy oil and soy protein for what they called "soy patriotism" (大豆報國)" (Honen Oil 1944, 3). This was the case not only for the soy-industry. Yoshihara Oil, which mainly handled non-soy oils, such as rapeseed oil and cottonseed oil, recognized that the Japanese vegetable oil industry had developed, thanks to military demands since Japan's modernization. Yoshihara Oil also traded castor oil, an important lubricant for machines and engines, to the Japanese Army and Navy (Hirano 1973, 54).

By the 1940s, soy had become indispensable to Japan: "Soy and war are indivisible. Soy is an essential resource in both peacetime and wartime" (Masuno 1942, 1). Honen Oil, one of the original components of today's dominant edible oil company, J-Oil Mills, wrote that the soy oil industry "had developed into a world-level large-scale industry that supplies raw materials to food, feed, fertilizer, fermenting, confectionary, medical, painting, soap, and other non-food and military manufacturing" (Honen Oil 1944, 1). In the 1940s, soy and other oil crops came under the management of the Japanese military, as Chapter 4 will demonstrate in detail.

Discussion

Once they had established soy-crushing as a large-scale capital-intensive mechanical-industry, the oil-related companies desperately needed to expand soy's versatility to create new products to sell in any possible market in order to maintain both Japanese big business and Japan's colonial power.

Mass-produced soy oil and meal: Products and markets

Today, Japan's self-sufficiency rate for vegetable oil is about 2–3%, and a frequently offered explanation for why Japan imports so much soy and rapeseed is that people want to eat more oily food when their income increases. Yet the history shows that the soy-crushing and oil-refining industries had already established a large production capacity relying on the overseas oil crops before ordinary Japanese people began eating oily food. In fact, as foods, both soy oil and hardened oil were new for Japanese people, and there was no demand for them to begin with. When the export market for soy oil and the fertilizer market for soy meal shrank dramatically after WWI, the Japanese soy companies, which had invested heavily in large-scale mechanical factories, urgently needed to create new selling outlets large enough to match their established mass-production capacity for soy meal and soy oil. Thus, they poured enormous efforts into research and development to expand the versatility of soy and to create new soy products to sell in any possible market. They even found it a challenge to sell soy meal to the Japanese food market, although the nation had eaten whole soy bean products for centuries. Instead, the main markets that the modern soy-industry could expand into were non-food industrial manufacturing, including soy-based glues, plastics, and paints, among others. The concurrent advancement of oleochemical and protein science and technologies helped this process. As the technologies for manufacturing hardened oil became possible, solidified oil became a raw material for a widening range of oleochemical products. Along with these corporate efforts to create markets for their mass-produced soy products, a few edible soy oil products began to be sold in 1920s Japan. However, it was only after WWII that edible soy oil disseminated widely in the Japanese diet.

Soy and the "visible hands" of business and government

The oil-press and soap industries transformed from a work of craftmanship into a modern, capital- and resource-intensive big business led by university-educated technical experts and managers. The advanced oleo-chemical and protein technologies, more sophisticated machinery, and highly educated human resources required, and attracted, more capital investment. The technological development encouraged the consolidation of oil-related industries into comprehensive oleochemical and protein manufacturing business groups, which began producing a range of advanced bio-chemical products. Competitive market conditions and the post-WWI economic depression encouraged mergers and acquisitions, leading to the concentration of capital in a few dominant companies. In addition to the existing *zaibatsu* like Mitsui and Mitsubishi, smaller but emerging *zaibatsu* around the interwar period actively invested in the chemical industries and military industries, forming the corporate groups known as *Konzern*. They took advantage of the increased military budget and the natural resources that came under the control of Japanese forces in the expanding Japanese empire, including Manchurian soy and Korean fish. The SMR Central Laboratory also worked to maximize the use of natural resources in Manchuria by developing the related industries for the benefit of Japan.

The point to note here is that many of these big business survived to post-WWII era, and they became main players that supplied edible oil products in peacetime food markets.

The role of soy in food and capitalist history: Making soy flexible between the Food Regimes

Such concentrated industries were easily integrated into military complexes. As Japan pursued its wars in Asia and the Pacific, soy-related big businesses became embedded in important military complexes under the Japanese government. At the time, bio-based oil and protein materials were important for military supplies, especially for Japan, which lacked petroleum resources. This was also the transitional period between the First and Second Food Regimes. As we have seen, soy was being made into a "flex crop," a very versatile and important commodity for economic, political, and military purpose, which enabled it to become a key commodity of the following Second Food Regime under US hegemony. The United States increased its own cultivation of soy and manufacturing of soy oil and meal domestically, especially in the 1930s. By the time WWII ended, the United States had become the main world supplier of soy, replacing Manchuria.

Note

1 MSG was invented by a Japanese in 1907 out of kelp, and the company began its production in 1908. "Ajinomoto" was a product name, and the company that manufactured it was initially called Suzuki (a common family name in Japan), but is unrelated to Suzuki Shoten. The company was renamed Ajinomoto only after WWII. To avoid confusion, I refer to the company as "Ajinomoto," without reflecting the change of company names over time.

Bibliography

In Japanese (with English translation by the author)

Ajinomoto (1971) *The History of Ajinomoto (before WW2)* (味の素株式会社社史編纂室 [1971]『味の素株式会社社史 1』（戦前編）味の素).

Hirano, S. (1973) *The Life Story of Yoshihara Sadajiro (Yoshihara Oil)* (平野成子 [1973]『油ひとすじ: 吉原定次郎翁伝』吉原製油株式会社).

Honen Oil (1944) *The Corporate History 20 Years* (豊年製油[1944]『豊年製油株式會社二十年史』豊年製油).

Honen Oil (1963) *The Corporate History 40 Years* (豊年製油株式会社 [1963]『豊年製油株式会社四十年史』豊年製油).

JOPA (Japan Oilseed Processors Association) (1972) *The History of Oil Industry* (日本油脂工業会 [1972]『油脂工業史』日本油脂工業会).

Kao Soap (1940) *The Corporate History 50 Years* (花王石鹸五十年史編纂委員会 [1940]『花王石鹸五十年史』花王石鹸五十年史編纂委員会).

Kubota, S. (1929) "On the Industry of Hardened-oil", *Journal of the Society of Chemical Industry, Japan* (久保田四郎 [1929]「硬化油工業に就て」『工業化学雑誌』32(4), pp. 392–398).

Kubota, S. (1937) "On the Industry of Glycerin", *Journal of the Society of Chemical Industry, Japan* (久保田四郎 [1937]「グリセリン工業に就て」『工業化学雑誌』40(5), pp. 372–379).

Masuno, M. (1942) *Soybean and Its Industry in the World* (増野實 [1942]『世界の大豆と工業』河出書房).

Mitsubishi Corporation (1986) *History of Mitsubishi Corporation ver.1* (三菱商事 [1986]『三菱商事社史 上』三菱商事株式会社).

Murayama, T. (1941) *Oil Industry in the World and Japan's National Policy on Oil* (村山威士 [1941]『世界油脂工業の趨勢と我が油脂国策』工政会).

Nakajima, T. ed. (1967) *History of Industrial Development in Modern Japan: Food Industry* (中島常雄 編 [1967]『現代日本産業発達史 第18食品』現代日本産業発達史研究会).

Nisshin Oil (1969) *The Corporate History 60 Years* (日清製油株式会社 [1969]『日清製油60年史』日清製油).

NOF (Nippon Oil & Fats Co.) (1967) *The Corporate History 30 Years* (日本油脂社史編纂委員会 [1967]『日本油脂三十年史』日本油脂株式会社).

Ooura, M. and Hirano, S. eds. (1948) *Golden Flower: The History of Japan Oil Company* (大浦万吉・平野茂之 編 [1948]『黄金の花: 日本製油株式会社沿革史（改訂増補版）』新潮社).

Sakaguchi, M. (2003) "The Bean Cake Market of Modern Japan" *Rikkyo Economic Review* (坂口誠 [2003]「近代日本の大豆粕市場: 輸入肥料の時代」立教経済学研究 57(2), pp. 53–70).
Sasama, Y. (1979) *The History of Japan's Food Industry* (笹間愛史 [1979]『日本食品工業史』東洋経済新報社).
Shibagaki, K. (1968) *One Hundred Years of Mitsui and Mitsubishi* (柴垣和夫 [1968]『三井・三菱の百年: 日本資本主義と財閥』中央公論社).
SMR (South Manchuria Railway) (1924a) *On Soy Processing* (南満洲鉄道株式会社農務課 [1924]『大豆の加工』（産業資料 其21）満蒙文化協会。
SMR (South Manchuria Railway) (1924b) *On Oil-Press Industry in Manchuria* (南満州鉄道株式会社庶務部調査課 [1924] 『滿洲に於ける油坊業』（滿鐵調査資料 第23編）南滿洲鐵道株式會社庶務部調査課).
Sugiyama, K. (1957) *My History (Sugiyama Kintaro)* (杉山金太郎 [1957]「杉山金太郎 私の履歴書」日本経済新聞社編『私の履歴書』（第4集）日本経済新聞社、pp. 143–179).
Taiwan Daily News (1938) (『台湾日日新報』1938.5.27）.
Takahashi, K. and Aoyama, J. (1938) *The Study of Japanese Zaibatsu* (高橋亀吉・青山二郎 [1938]『日本財閥論』（日本コンツエルン全書 第1）春秋社).
Tamaki, H. (1976) *The History of Japanese Zaibatsu* (玉城肇 [1976]『日本財閥史』社会思想社).
Tokyo Oil Wholesaler Market (2000) *The History of Tokyo Oil Wholesalers* (東京油問屋市場 [2000]『東京油問屋史：油商のルーツを訪ねる』東京油問屋市場).
Tsujimoto, M. (1916) *Japanese Vegetable Oils* (辻本満丸 [1916]『日本植物油脂』丸善).

Websites

Business Archives Online (丸善企業史料統合データベース; for business reports of related companies) https://j-dac.jp/bao, Japan Digital Archives Center.
Kobe University Digital Archive Newspaper Clippings Collection (神戸大学附属図書館 デジタルアーカイブ) www.lib.kobe-u.ac.jp/sinbun/, Kobe University.
NDL Digital Collections (国立国会図書館デジタルコレクション) https://dl.ndl.go.jp/, National Diet Library (Japan).
North China Railway Archive https://codh.rois.ac.jp/north-china-railway/, The North China Railway Archive Committee, and the Center for Open Data in the Humanities (CODH).
Oil History Archive (東京油問屋市場「油歴史資料館」) www.abura.gr.jp, The Tokyo Oil Wholesaler Market.
Suzuki Shoten Memorial Museum (鈴木商店記念館) www.suzukishoten-museum.com, Suzukishoten-museum.

4 Shifting to edible oil and American soy (before, during, and after WWII)

From "important war industry" to food industry

Introduction

As we have seen, Japanese oil-related big business developed by crushing Manchurian soy and other Asian oil crops, mainly producing industrial raw materials for non-food manufacturing and military supplies, rather than for food uses. With the large capital investment of old and new *zaibatsu*, the oil-related companies built large-scale mechanical factories near the port districts in Japan and in Manchuria; these so-called "sea factories" were convenient for importing their raw materials and exporting their mass-produced products. This physical infrastructure helped the same companies maintain flexibility. Thus, after WWII, they were able to pivot to using US soy rather than Asian oil crops and to shift from selling supplies to the military to a new focus on the food market. Moreover, the advantages that large companies enjoyed during the war as providers of important military supplies (e.g., special allotments of raw materials, permission to build new production facilities, and access to new technology and human resources) had effects that carried over after Japan's defeat. Hence, many of these companies were able to quickly restart and refocus their businesses, and several of them grew to become the dominant food companies in post-WWII Japan.

The Asian oil crops that supported the Japanese oleochemical industries

Although it was Manchurian soy that gave the initial boost to the Japanese soy-crushing companies (Honen Oil 1944, 20), Japan used other Asian oil crops as well. Yoshihara Oil, which mainly handled non-soy oils, relied for more than 90% of its raw materials on imports from Manchuria and China. According to its corporate history, "the Japanese vegetable oil industry could develop this far all thanks to having the natural treasure house of oil crops in the Chinese continent nearby" (Hirano 1973, 98). The Japanese dependence on Asian oil crops at the beginning of the 1940s is clear from

DOI: 10.4324/9781032678733-5

the following figures, compiled by a researcher in the industry: 100% of soy bean, perilla, and hempseed came from Manchuria; 75% of cottonseed came from China and 17% from Manchuria; 65% of castor bean came from Manchuria and 15% from British India; 100% of rapeseed came from China; 70% of sesame came from China and 25% from Manchuria; 90% of groundnut came from Manchuria and 10% from China; 67% of linseed came from China, 25% from Iraq, and 8% from Manchuria and British India; and 90% of copra came from the Dutch East Indies and 10% from the Philippines and elsewhere (Murayama 1941, 24).

In fact, Asia was the global supplier of vegetable oils and oil crops before WWII, when bio-based oil and protein materials were crucial for a wide range of industries. The Commonwealth Economic Committee (CEC 1948) estimated that the Asian regions that Japan occupied during the war had supplied about 40%, or nearly half, of the world's vegetable oils and oil crops. The area included the Philippine archipelago (mainly supplying copra and coconut oil), Malaya and the Dutch East Indies (palm fruit and palm kernel), and China and Manchuria (soy bean, rapeseed, and other oil crops); in addition, Japan produced fish oil from the seas surrounding the Korean peninsula and Japan.

It is difficult to accurately trace how much of which oil crops were used for which oleochemical products, because oils and fats can be sourced from a wide range of plants and animals as well as petroleum, and the continued advances in oleochemical technologies around this time made it ever-easier to substitute one for another. (For example, margarine has been made from beef tallow, whale oil, cottonseed oil, soy oil, and palm oil, according to time and circumstance.) Corporate histories, however, offer a general idea of which raw materials were favored in modernizing Japan. The soap industry used mainly imported beef tallow and coconut oil in the Meiji era, and then shifted to hardened oil from various oil crops in the 1920s and 1930s, and to synthetic soap and detergents in the post-WWII era (Kao Soap 1940). The hardened oil industry was based on cheap fish oil at the beginning, but, as we saw in Chapter 3, shifted to soy oil when it was targeted by the soy-crushing companies as a new market. In 1922, the Ministry of Agriculture and Industry (農商務省) reported that "the raw materials to manufacture hardened oil are soy oil and fish oil. When fish oil becomes short, soy oil can supplement it" (125). UENO Seiichi, an expert in the industry, said that soy oil was often used to manufacture hardened oil in Dalian (Manchuria), but fish oil was cheaper for the manufacturers in Japan, who turned to soy oil only when it became more economical (Ueno 1927).

The raw materials for glycerin are particularly difficult to trace, because it is a more sophisticated oleochemical product, an alcohol, that can be processed from a wide range of oils and fats. In the 1930s, KUBOTA Shiro, another expert in oleochemical technology and also an industry leader, wrote that fish-oil-based hardened oil, whale oil, soy oil, coconut oil, beef tallow, and soy-oil-based hardened oil were possible raw materials for manufacturing glycerin in Japan (Kubota 1937). Glycerin itself is an intermediate commodity that can be a raw material in a wide range of products in food and non-food industries, including medicine as well as explosives like dynamite. In addition, Kubota claimed that "there is no such thing as a glycerin industry" because glycerin was often manufactured as a by-product of the soap industry and oil-related industries (Kubota 1937). For example, in the United Kingdom, about 95% of glycerin produced originated from the soap industry (Kao Soap 1940, 82–83, 116, 390, 514). In Japan, Kao Soap was recovering glycerin from wastewater from soap manufacturing in 1911, and according to Kao's corporate history, it used a method that had been developed in Europe by the end of the 19th century (Kao Soap 1940, 82–83, 116, 390, 514).

Big business in the oil and oleochemical industries during the interwar period

The Japanese economy, in general, suffered a downturn after WWI and throughout the Great Depression. For a few bigger oil companies that survived the hard times, however, the business environment actually improved after the Manchurian Incident of 1931. "In contrast to the tense general social situation, the Japanese vegetable oil industry gathered steam with unprecedentedly good business" in the 1930s, according to a biography of YOSHIHARA Sadajiro, the founder of Yoshihara Oil. His company was exporting rapeseed oil, cottonseed oil, and perilla oil, as well as cottonseed meal and linseed meal, much of it to the United States (Yoshihara Oil Business Report for October 1934–March 1935), reaching their top volume of vegetable oil exports in 1935 (Hirano 1973, 70), as shown in Table 4.1.

Table 4.1 Yoshihara Oil exports in its peak year of 1935

	Export volume (kg)	*Export value (US$)*
Rapeseed oil	5,936,076	781,660
Perilla oil	7,600,027	1,119,797
Cottonseed oil	5,473,230	631,715
Kapok oil	408,240	50,381
Castor oil	36,288	5,407
Mustard oil	45,360	5,300
Corn oil	54,432	8,130
Poppy seed oil	5,443	954
Total	19,559,096	2,603,344

Source: Adapted from Hirano (1973, 78).

The Japanese domestic demand for vegetable oil also grew to some degree, though almost entirely in non-food markets. The demand from military supply industries and chemical and machine industries rapidly increased as Japan expanded its battlefields in China. Yoshihara Oil, which originated as an oil trader in Osaka, rapidly expanded its business operations in this period, not only in trading but also in oil-refining, for which the company built four more factories in Japan (Hirano 1973, 70–95).

In soy oil production, Honen Oil, with its foundation in Manchurian soy, had become the dominant company, producing about 60–70% of Japan's soy oil by volume in those days (Table 4.2). In the rapidly developing field of oleochemical processing, several companies consolidated, with investment from the emerging *zaibatsu*. Among them, the Nissan *Konzern* actively bought up companies and integrated them into Nippon Oil, which manufactured more than half (57%) of the hardened oil produced in Japan (NOF 1967, 178).

Further consolidation of the oleochemical industry in the wartime economy

As the wartime economy subsumed Japan, many industries were reorganized. The oleochemical industries, in particular, had a crucial role in modern

Table 4.2 The share of Honen Oil in Japanese soy oil production, 1924–1939

	Soy oil production in Japan (volume, ton)	*By Honen Oil*	
		Volume (ton)	*Percentage (%)*
1924	23,611	16,987	**71.9**
1925	35,985	24,024	**66.8**
1926	39,734	27,917	**70.3**
1927	33,319	23,800	**71.4**
1928	38,406	26,701	**69.5**
1929	43,590	32,872	**75.3**
1930	39,689	28,459	**71.7**
1931	46,883	35,726	**76.2**
1932	51,531	29,383	**57.0**
1933	44,448	29,897	**67.3**
1934	51,467	38,220	**74.3**
1935	42,899	29,865	**70.0**
1936	47,943	38,253	**79.8**
1937	51,343	38,034	**74.1**
1938	67,000	43,118	**64.3**
1939	66,879	40,237	**60.2**

Source: Adapted from Honen Oil (1993, 33).

Note: Bold values are emphasis by the author.

warfare, and the oligopoly structure of the businesses that had controlled large part from soy-crushing to advanced oleochemical processing by then became further consolidated as a wartime institution under government and military management. In April 1931, soon after the Manchurian Incident, the Act for the Control of Important Industries (重要産業統制令) was issued. The oleochemical companies that manufactured hardened oil were designated an "important war industry" and consolidated into the Japan Hardened Oil Association (日本硬化油同業会) in September 1931. This association became an institution to control companies that manufactured hardened oils, fatty acids, glycerin, soap, oil solutions, and synthetic detergents. Their procurement of raw materials (mainly fish oil from occupied Korea), manufacturing, research and development, and the delivery and sale of their products were all managed through this wartime structure（JFOA 1972, 72–73).

After Japan attacked Pearl Harbor and began the Pacific War in 1941, the government's control of the oil and oleochemical industries tightened further. The government urged smaller companies to consolidate into larger companies to make the industry more efficient. In the following year, 1942, all the oil-related companies were consolidated into two institutions: the plant- and animal-based oil-processing companies were gathered into the Imperial Oil Crop Management Company (帝国油糧統制株式会社) under the Ministry of Agriculture and Forestry, and the oleochemical companies that manufactured hardened oil, hardened wax, fatty acids, and other advanced oleochemical products became the Oil and Fat Association (油脂統制会) under the Ministry of Commerce and Industries. These wartime industrial associations collaborated with the government to execute wartime policies（JFOA 1972, 141–151). In addition, every plant-, animal-, and fish-based oil and oil crop, including soy and rapeseed, was brought under the integrated management of the Ministry of Agriculture and Forestry (Honen Oil 1963, 61). The executive members of the large oil companies, like Honen Oil, Nippon Oil, and the companies related to Suzuki Shoten were gathered to manage these wartime organizations（NOF 1967, 176, 18; Nishikawa 1942, 381–382).

The important point to notice here is that these big businesses, which were consolidated into a military institution, continued their R&D and production operations during the war, under military orders and protection, as an important war industry. The edge they thus gained during the war enabled them to swiftly transform into food companies after 1945 (Kao Soap 1960).

The large companies' continued operation as munitions manufacturers

In the wartime economy, the large oil and oleochemical companies were ordered to manufacture munitions and war-supporting products. The raw materials were supplied on a priority basis by military order, and the factories continued R&D and production throughout the war. As importing petroleum became difficult, Japan became more desperate to utilize the oil crops produced in Asia, and the oil-related companies were ordered to manufacture substitutes for petroleum products from these bio-based oils and meals. Especially important to develop and manufacture was aviation oil, the lubricant used for combat planes. More than a thousand experts and engineers were mobilized for more than five years for such research and development projects.

Yoshihara Oil, now a designated manufacturer for the Japanese Army and Navy, "became very busy processing castor oil for aviation oil, rapeseed oil for steel hardening oil, and other oleochemical products. We were able to make plenty of profits, enough to supplement the reduced exports because of the war" (Hirano 1973, 97). Nippon Oil and Kao Soap also conducted research and development related to aviation oil. Kao Soap began building a new factory under a Navy order during the war, but the factory exploded during its test operation in 1944, the year before Japan was defeated. A kind of biofuel, fatty acid ethyl ester, was developed from coconut oil and soy oil as well (Nippon Oil 1967; Kao Soap 1993). Although the innovation of manufacturing aviation oil out of plant-based oil was praised as a great achievement during the war, actual production was limited, and its contribution to Japan's wartime successes is questionable. Still, an expert reflecting on this achievement noted that "at least, young engineers and experts were able to gain precious experience in basic research, industrial implementation research, building of factories and operating them. This is an intangible asset" (KAWAKAMI Yasota in Kao Soap 1960, 99–100).

During the war, Ajinomoto (the MSG company) began producing a wide range of chemicals, such as butanol and acetone, and chemical products like hydrolyzed vegetable protein, acidum hydrochloricum, and fertilizers, utilizing its knowledge and technologies to manufacture these from plant-based raw materials like sugar and sweet potatoes. The company later claimed that it had to collaborate in the manufacture of munitions to avoid becoming the target of a merger, which is why "our company transformed from a food company into a munitions factory after 1943" (Ajinomoto 1971, 405). The new factory the company built in Kyushu during the war to manufacture such military chemical products later became one of their production bases in the post-WWII era (Ajinomoto 1971).

In fact, even before WWII reached the Pacific, Japan was facing growing challenges in international trade. The United States raised tariffs on the importation of vegetable oils in 1935. This was a devastating change for Japanese oil companies. According to a Nisshin Oil business report,

> the American government imposed such a high tariff as to almost ban the import of vegetable oil, and this move was like a bolt from the blue for

> Japanese oil companies, which had expanded their production capacity with the US as the biggest trading partner in the previous three to four years.
>
> (Nisshin Oil "Business Report" for FY August 1936 to July 1937)

It also became more difficult to obtain oil crops even within the Asian region, as Japan lost more and more ships and workers in the wars. By then, the military-government was managing all the oil crops, including rapeseed and castor, as important munitions resources, so oilseeds were "directly supplied to the designated munitions factories by the military, and other factories in civil sectors received only a small volume of remaining materials" (Nisshin Oil 1969, 173). A business report of Nisshin Oil reveals that the company made certain profits by using half of its Yokohama and Dalian factories to produce munitions supplies, for which the company received benefits as a government-designated munitions manufacturer (Nisshin Oil "Business Report" from August 1937 to July 1938). Thus, the company managed to continue operations by producing castor oil and other oil and fat products for military supplies; the military and domestic demand offset the damage of sluggish exports (Nisshin Oil 1969, 165, 170). Honen Oil was also designated a munitions company in 1944 and increased its soy-processing volume from 1942 to 1944, maintaining an annual processing volume of 240,000 tons, despite a soy shortage at the height of WWII (Honen Oil 1963, 62; Honen Oil 1993, 62). Both Nisshin Oil and Honen Oil were dominant oil companies that had factories in Dalian, and they continued increasing production while working with and for Manchukuo, the puppet-state of Japan.

According to their business reports, Honen Oil, Nisshin Oil, and Yoshihara Oil recorded continuous profits during the wartime period from 1931 to 1945. The reports also express appreciation for support from Manchukuo and the nationalistic desire to work for the nation, indicating that these dominant companies continued active operation for military purposes while having close relationships with the government and military. While the large companies saw gains from running designated munitions factories, smaller oil factories that pressed domestic oil crops were wiped out, as "the government policy was so focused on securing the absolute volume of oil and fat that it concentrated on the sea factories and almost forgot about subsidies and supportive policies for the small-scale mountain factories" (Japan Oil News 1949, 57). In other words, wartime policies cleared away small-scale oil mills and concentrated the oil-related industries into a few hands for military purposes.

As the war continued, Japan seized large parts of Southeast Asia that included Dutch and British oil crop plantations, mainly of coconut and oil palm, along with oil-pressing factories. The government appointed Japanese oil companies, Honen Oil, Yoshihara Oil, and Settsu Oil, to manage these oil resources for the benefit of Japan (Honen Oil 1963, 48; Hirano 1973, 95). Imports of tropical oils to Japan surged briefly; however, the military situation soon deteriorated, and Japan's defeat came before it could fully utilize these tropical oil resources.

The postwar shift of resources and markets

Japan was defeated in 1945, and the Japanese oil and oleochemical industries lost their major sources of oil crops in Manchuria, Korea, and Southeast Asia, as well as their munitions market. Although they had lost overseas factories and assets, the big companies maintained the large domestic production capacity that they had continued to develop during the war, and now they became desperate to find raw materials to feed their oversized factories. The oil companies, the industry associations, and the government, all struggled to locate raw materials; so they tried to promote import, as well as to increase domestic production, or to find less utilized oil resources in order to gather enough raw materials of any kind soon after the war-end (JOPA 1963, 18).

Government control of input and output to the advantage of big business

After Japan was defeated, international trade, including of oil crops, was controlled by the US-led occupation government until January 1950. The allocation of raw materials was also managed by the government; thus, despite the change in national governance from wartime to peacetime, deciding which company would receive what and how much raw material remained a political issue (JOPA 1963, 28).

The General Headquarters of the Supreme Commander for the Allied Powers (SCAP) gave orders in 1946 that the occupation government should directly manage important raw materials and essential goods for the nation, including food and oil resources (JOPA 1963, 15). Although Japan's wartime institutional structure was dismantled, a new government institution was established in 1948 to manage the entire oil industry. The Oil and Oil Crop Distribution Public Corporation (油糧配給公団) was fully funded by the government and supervised by the Ministry of Agriculture and Forestry (Nakajima ed. 1967, 527; JOPA 1963, 11–16). In other words, the Japanese oil industry remained under government management even after the war, and the peacetime national policies still favored the larger oil companies, claiming the need for efficiency. The Public Corporation allocated the scarce oil crops to the larger companies based on their production capacity; it also bought up all of their products and then supplied them to the market at a certain price. This system secured markets and certain profits for the assigned companies (Nakajima ed. 1967, 528), encouraging the big oil companies to further increase their production capacity, which was already overextended far beyond the demands of the domestic market (Japan Oil News 1949, 55).

The swift postwar recovery of the dominant oil companies

The dominant oil companies that had run the wartime-designated munitions factories soon recovered under the new government's management. They had lost their assets overseas (especially in Manchuria), and their domestic facilities had received some damage from air attacks (although some of them had been evacuated to safer places by military order). Nevertheless, at a time when most of Japanese society was suffering from the damages of war and the lack of all materials, these big oleochemical companies still had sufficient facilities to maintain a large production capacity and even some stocks of raw materials.

Within a few years after the war's end, these companies sought new sources of raw materials to feed their oversized factories. Table 4.3 shows the production capacity of main companies and their low levels of actual production (as a percentage of full capacity) in 1948.

American soy replaces Manchurian soy

Immediately after the defeat, the Japanese government urgently promoted domestic cultivation of food and oilseeds, including soy and rapeseed. But what actually saved the Japanese oil companies was the American soy beans imported as relief aid through the US Government Appropriation for Relief in Occupied Areas (GARIOA). An industry history claimed that "the oil industry recovered thanks to the import of GARIOA soy beans. This resulted in soy oil becoming the largest of the edible oil industries in Japan" (Nakajima ed. 1967, 528). US soy bean imports increased rapidly: from 1,582 tons in 1946 to 15,306 tons in 1947, to 49,458 tons in 1948, and to 190,186 tons in 1949. Honen Oil, which had been the dominant soy-crusher in Japan, received most of this raw material, processing 782 tons in 1946, 7,630 tons in 1947, 26,525 tons in 1948, and 82,688 tons in 1949 (Honen Oil 1993, 74).

Honen Oil had lost their Dalian factory, but the company's production data show that, although total production volume plunged from a peak of over 300,000 tons in 1934 to a low of 782 tons in 1946, it recovered swiftly to process 26,525 tons in 1948 and 82,688 tons in 1949 (Table 4.4; Honen Oil 1963, 109). According to Honen Oil, after the company lost the supply of Manchurian soy beans, "we had to depend on the US soy beans from GARIOA" (Honen Oil 1963, 91).

Table 4.3 The ratio of actual production to production capacity of the large oil companies in 1948

	Monthly processing capacity	*Monthly average processing volume*	*The actual operation ratio (%)*	*Main raw materials*	*Factory location*
Honen Oil	18,016	2,426.5	13.47	Soy	Shimizu in Shizuoka Prefecture (Naruo factory was closed till 1949)
Nikka Oil	13,621	1,695.7	12.45	Soy, copra, peanut	Wakamatsu in Fukuoka Prefecture
Ajinomoto	8,680	1,063.4	12.25	Soy	Yokohama in Kanagawa Prefecture
Yoshihara Oil	8,841	845.2	9.56	Copra, peanut, linseed	Nishinomiya in Hyogo Prefecture
Showa Sangyo	4,176	517.6	12.39	Soy	Yokohama in Kanagawa Prefecture
Settsu Oil	3,188	484.1	15.19	Copra, peanut, linseed, castor	Osaka in Osaka Fu.
Nisshin Oil	896	229.0	25.56	Soy, copra, linseed, peanut	Nasu in Tochigi Prefecture

Source: Compiled by the author based on data from Japan Oil News (1949, 59), with location notes added by the author from corporate histories and business reports.

Honen Oil showed its gratitude by holding a grand "Soy Bean Festival" to welcome the first American cargo ship that brought a GARIOA soy bean shipment from the United States to its factory's Shimizu port in May 1948. A corporate history reported this event as follows:

> The first cargo ship after the end of war came to Shimizu Factory dock on May 3rd, 1948, with 8,300 tons of US soy beans. It was the first full-scale soy import since the war ended, which Japanese companies were craving. To welcome this soy cargo ship, Honen Oil company held a special "Soy Bean Festival." About 300 high-ranking people attended this event, including the executive officers from GHQ, the Minister of Agriculture and Forestry, and the members of the Upper and Lower Houses of Japan's Diet, as well as other important people in business, bureaucracy, and the government.
>
> (Honen Oil 1993, 75)

Table 4.4 Soy-processing volume of Honen Oil during and after WWII, 1941–1960 (unit: ton)

	Shimizu factory	*Naruo factory*	*Dalien factory*	*Total*
1941	99,930	44,927	36,620	181,477
1942	105,443	45,485	93,142	244,070
1943	89,332	43,621	107,638	240,591
1944	96,759	31,278	114,105	242,142
1945	34,076	8,647	56,320	99,043
1946	**782**			**782**
1947	**7,630**			**7,630**
1948	**26,525**			**26,525**
1949	**82,337**	361		**82,698**
1950	59,563	14,859		74,422
1951	34,371	17,935		52,306
1952	33,669	21,499		55,168
1953	48,317	31,671		79,988
1954	43,469	26,577		70,046
1955	58,270	26,705		84,975
1956	62,462	30,245		92,707
1957	65,497	29,584		95,081
1958	73,396	30,643		104,039
1959	91,397	38,271		129,668
1960	103,041	47,377		150,418

Source: Adapted from Honen Oil (1963, 109), with the total figures calculated by the author.

Note: Bold values are emphasis by the author.

As this episode suggests, the Japanese oil industry relied heavily on US soy for their recovery and their future growth in the post-WWII era.

Another dominant soy-crushing company, Nisshin Oil, suffered more damage during the war. It lost over 90% of its assets, including its main Dalian factory in Manchuria. In addition, its Yokohama factory was burned and the land was taken over by the occupying army. Yet the company had also built a few inland factories by military order during the war, and it had evacuated some production facilities to these sites. Utilizing these wartime legacy facilities, Nisshin Oil began pressing oil from remaining stocks of castor seed and copra, its allocation of GARIOA soy beans, and any domestic seeds it could find that were available in Japan, such as the seeds of Chinese cabbage, Japanese radish, and squashes. The company managed to begin selling salad oil and tempura oil in 1949.

Nippon Oil, the largest oleochemical company during the war, received rather modest damage, and the condition of its factories in Ooji, Tsukuda, and Amagasaki enabled it to restart operations soon. It also had about 30,000 remaining tons of crude oil stocks, enough to support production for about one year. In 1946, the year following Japan's defeat, Nippon Oil accounted for market shares of 28% for margarine, 23% for soap, and 15% for hardened oil in Japan (NOF 1967, 249).

In this way, the Japanese big oil and oleochemical companies recovered rather swiftly, and they became the welcoming receivers of US soy beans when the United States wanted to increase its soy exports.

The United States' creation of overseas markets for American commodities

When Japan lost its overseas territories, it lost the strongholds of Asian oil crop resources in Manchuria, China, and Southeast Asia, on which the Japanese oil and oleochemical industries had relied heavily for their development. After the war's end, the occupation government controlled Japan's international trade, including soy and oil crops. The trade statistics show some imports of soy beans from the United States and China as early as 1946 (Table 4.5), and imports of US soy increased steadily through the

Table 4.5 Postwar soy imports to Japan from the United States and China, 1948–1963 (unit: tons)

	From US	*From China*	*Related events*
1946	1,582	-	
1947	10,516	4,790	
1948	30,409	13,866	The government-funded Oil and Oil Crop Distribution Public Corporation started
1949	147,680	40,830	The People's Republic of China is established
1950	94,994	102,116	Korean War broke out
1951	301,929	4,551	The control on soy and rapeseed was released and shifted to an automatic approval system (AA system)
1952	161,874	386	The war chaotic situation led to the repeal of AA system in 1953
1953	408,704	16,940	Shift to planned import system based on the Act on Stabilization of the Price of Agricultural Crops and the foreign currency quota system (1953–1961)
1954	442,874	45,864	The US PL480
1955	569,907	203,521	
1956	536,055	165,790	
1957	604,359	199,607	
1958	777,436	98,197	
1959	951,232	-	
1960	1,091,364	147	
1961	1,101,933	42,490	Deregulation of soy import (shift to AA system)
1962	1,125,799	165,020	
1963	1,314,303	226,644	

Source: Adapted from Food Agency *The Oil-Crop Statistics Yearbook* (1963, 188–189), with the notes of related events added by the author.

1950s, although the trade deregulation of 1961 is often regarded as the trigger for Japan becoming a major importer of US soy beans.

Food aid played a significant role in increasing exports of US commodities. After WWI, the United States began exporting its agricultural commodities to European countries as food aid, and at one time, food aid accounted for over 70% of US commodity exports. After WWII, food aid was part of the Marshall Plan projects for Europe and the United Nations projects for defeated areas and developing countries, and it became even more important for absorbing America's overproduced commodities. In the 1950s, as European countries recovered from the war and began producing ample amounts of food themselves, the surplus US commodities needed to find other overseas markets. Thus, the Agricultural Trade Development and Assistance Act of 1954 (so-called PL480) was established to further solidify the export structure of US commodities to overseas markets in peacetime commercial trade (Clapp 2012).

Japan was one of the export destinations for these US commodities. Some previous literature assumed the US strategy of expanding overseas markets for their surplus grains and oilseeds, including soy bean and oil, using food aid export strategies, and this impacted the recipient nations' diet and food self-sufficiency (Sekishita, 1987; Friedmann and McMichael 1989). The recent research, however, began to reveal that there had been more complicated negotiations among multiple government offices for different kinds of grains around the Mutual Security Act (MSA) in 1951 and PL-480 in 1955 (Ito 2021 and his other works). Also, some reluctance of US farmers in increasing soy production instead of the government effort for promoting soy cultivation has been revealed (Prodöhl 2023). The actual situation of increasing soy cultivation and their purposes, and the Japanese side of receiving soy soon after war-end may be the future research topic. Here, I just confirm the import of US soy bean significantly increased in post-WWII Japan with some political involvement in the 1950s before Japan deregulated import of soy in the early 1960s, and I focus on how Japanese side received those increased US soy.

Competition over US "concession soy"

The government-managed foreign trade of soy shifted to civil trade in January 1950, and control over the soy trade relaxed to some extent. It was strengthened again, however, to address chaotic trade and price situations caused by the Dodge Line economic policies and the outbreak of the Korean War at the beginning of the 1950s. In the end, a US dollar quota was imposed on soy bean imports in 1953, and thus the government continued to indirectly manage the allocation of imported soy bean among Japanese companies (JOPA 1963, 25–26; Nakajima ed. 1967, 531).

This indirect management system for imported soy caused severe competition over the limited supply. The government offices of the Ministry of International Trade, the Ministry of Agriculture and Forestry, the big oil businesses that mainly crushed imported oil crops, the smaller oil businesses that mainly crushed domestic crops, the growing livestock industry that used soy meal for feed, the manufacturers of glutamic acid, and the trading companies all competed with each other for a quota of the US soy. As soy beans became even more of a political issue, they received the epithet of "*riken* soy bean," meaning "concession (or rights, interests) soy beans" (JOPA 1963).

Once again, the larger oil companies had the advantage. For example, data on the allocation of imported soy beans for crushing in 1953 show that 20.4% went to Honen Oil, 14.1% to Ajinomoto, 10.5% to Nisshin Oil, and 9.9% to Nikka Oil. Thus, the top four companies secured more than half of the year's supply—and the top ten companies accounted for over 80% of it (Table 4.6) (Food Agency 1956, 73). Because the quota was decided based on production capacity, the oil companies invested in further expanding their capacity to volumes beyond the demand. The result was overproduction of soy oil. The large companies also persuaded the government to list oil and oleochemical manufacturing as important industries for Japan's post-WWII economic recovery, thus achieving some tax breaks for installing yet more production facilities (JOPA 1963, 33).

In reaction, smaller oil companies gathered and established the Japan Oil Crop Industry Cooperation Association (日本油糧工業協同組合連合会) to which they persuaded the government to allocate a certain amount of oil crops starting in 1955. While the smaller companies were criticized at the

Table 4.6 The allocation of imported soy beans in 1953

Company name	*Allocated volume (ton)*	*Percentage (%)*	*Accumulated percentage*
Honen Oil	48,411	20.4%	20.4%
Ajinomoto	33,289	14.1%	34.5%
Nisshin Oil	24,918	10.5%	45.0%
Nikka Oil	23,450	9.9%	54.9%
Showa Sangyo	22,377	9.4%	64.4%
Nippon Koyu	15,107	6.4%	70.7%
Fukoku Yushi	9,793	4.1%	74.9%
Yoshihara Oil	6,634	2.8%	77.7%
Kanegafuchi Chemical	6,152	2.6%	80.3%
Yokkaichi Mamekasu	5,666	2.4%	82.7%
Kumazawa Oil	4,694	2.0%	84.6%

Source: Adapted from Food Agency (1956, 73).

time for exploiting discourses about the need to protect small businesses and encourage domestic agriculture, the overall advantage remained with the larger oil companies (Nakajima ed. 1967, 533).

A detailed history of the political conflicts over imported soy beans is beyond the scope of this book. Focusing on the Japanese oil industries, however, two points are important. First, direct and indirect governmental control over the oil industries continued even after the war ended, and policies continued to favor larger oil companies. Second, the tendency of oversupply continued because the companies kept expanding, both as wartime military-designated companies and in response to the post-WWII competition over the quota allocation, rather than meet the consumer demand. Their mass-production structure required action to increase the sale of their products, as discussed more in Chapter 5.

Consolidation into larger factories in the port regions

In the 1950s and 1960s, Japan moved to a more open economy. The country participated in the 1955 General Agreement on Tariffs and Trade (GATT), and the government announced its plans for free trade and free exchange rates in 1960 (貿易為替自由化計画大綱). The import of oil crops also was deregulated for soy beans in 1961 and rapeseed in 1971.

Along with the deregulation of imported oil crops, the Japanese government encouraged the oil industry to intensify production by building larger facilities in the port regions, discouraging the smaller inland oil companies, which had been built in or near rural areas, mostly to crush domestic rapeseed. An industry history describes "the government's strong directive" at the time as follows:

> The government proposed the structural reform of the industry, by closing smaller oil factories inland as much as possible, and by only keeping the larger oil companies that could continue their business even after oil crop importation was fully deregulated. The government also requested the oil industry to bear the cost of this restructuring. As part of this restructuring policy, the nine larger oil companies raised funds of 27,197,000 yen to be paid to 81 smaller oil companies as consolation funds to close or change their business. The Japan Oil Crop Industry Cooperation Association, which consisted of many smaller oil companies, was dissolved in 1983.
>
> (JOPA 2012, 119)

As this incident demonstrates, the government actively engaged in political intervention to concentrate capital in the oil industry.

The intensification of oil production into larger factories in the port areas is confirmed by two sets of data. First, Figure 4.1 shows the change in the number of oil-crop-crushing factories according to production capacity. The smaller factories, those that produced less than 1 ton per year, had already been omitted from the statistics by 1961. Thus, from 1 ton to less than 10 tons per year is the smallest production size category in this dataset. There were over a thousand factories in this smallest category at the beginning of the 1960s, but within a decade the number was fewer than 100.

The second dataset concerns oil crop production capacity across Japanese prefectures in the decade between 1961 and 1970. As Figure 4.2 shows, many oil factories in inland prefectures closed, while in prefectures with large ports, oil-crushing volume increased. In 1961, Japan still produced a large amount of rapeseed, and 318,065 tons of rapeseed was crushed in

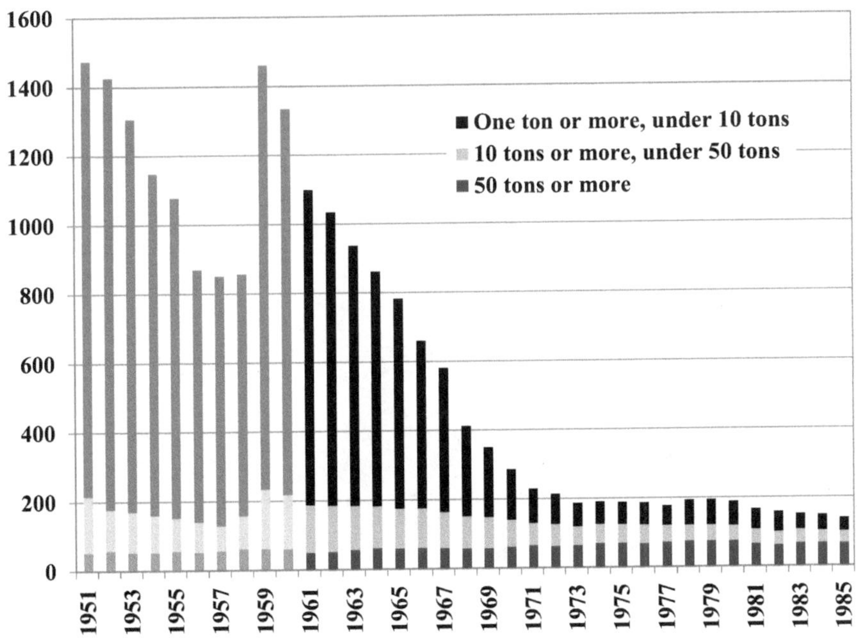

Figure 4.1 Numbers of oil crop-crushing factories by production capacity, 1951–1985.

Note: There was a change in calculation of the production capacity in 1960, thus the statistics has poor continuity. Nevertheless, this graph includes data before 1960 (in slightly gray) to indicate the significant number of factories in the decade following Japan's defeat in WWII.

Source: Produced by the author based on data from MAFF *The Situation of Oil-crop Industries* 1961, 1970, 1990–2001.

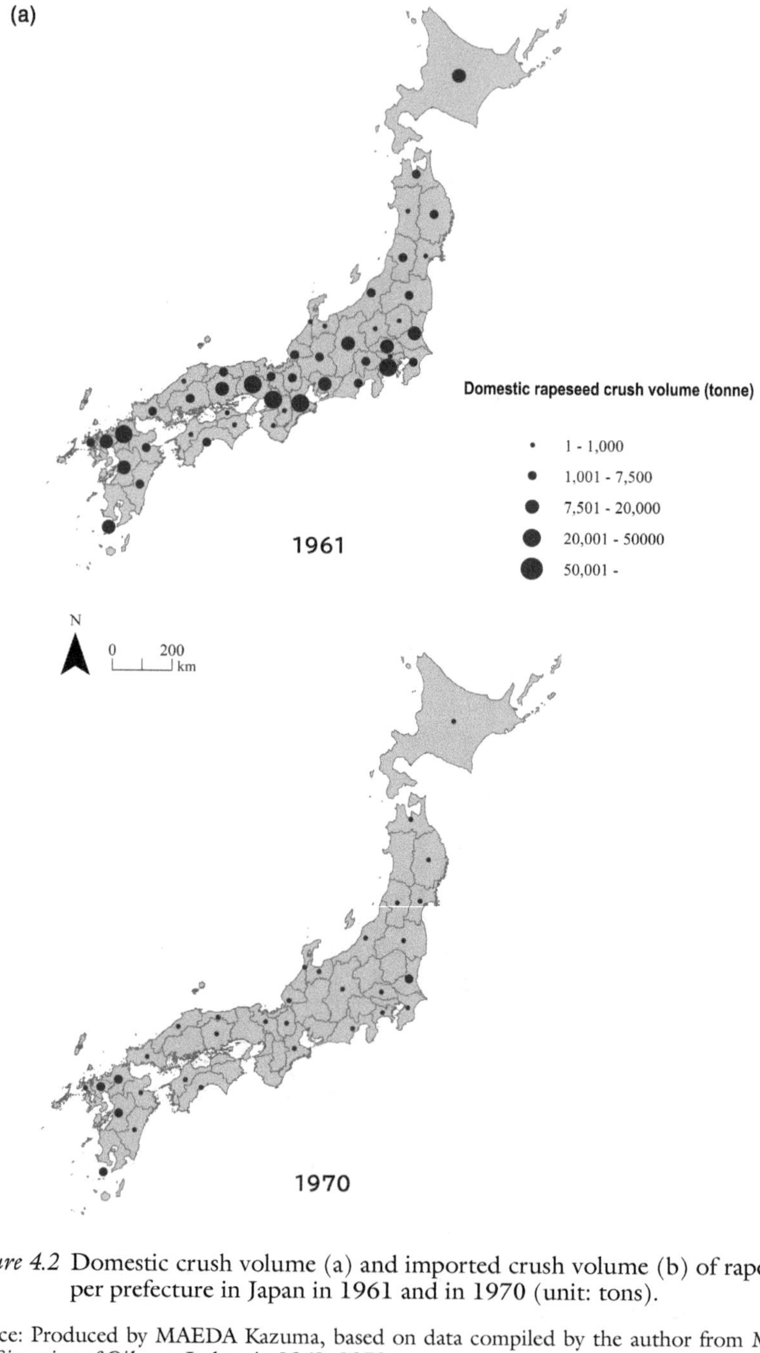

Figure 4.2 Domestic crush volume (a) and imported crush volume (b) of rapeseed per prefecture in Japan in 1961 and in 1970 (unit: tons).

Source: Produced by MAEDA Kazuma, based on data compiled by the author from MAFF *The Situation of Oil-crop Industries* 1961, 1970.

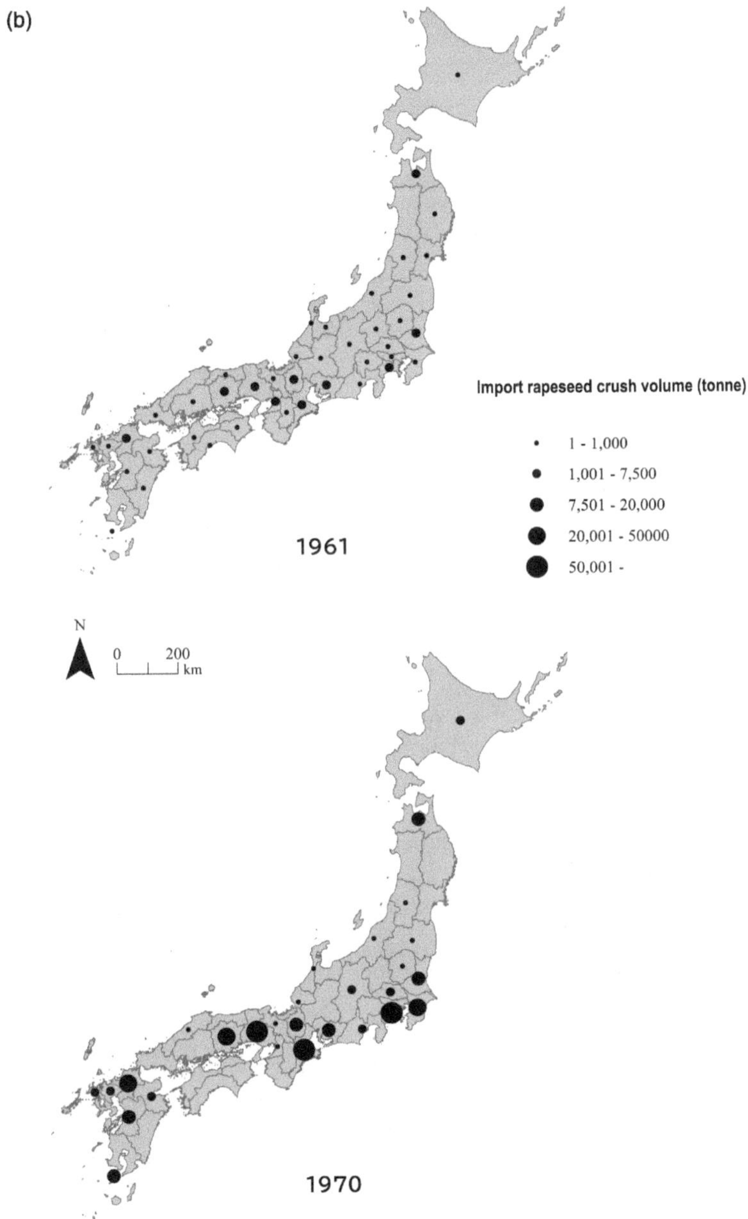

Figure 4.2 (Continued)

Table 4.7 Soy-processing volume in top prefectures in 1961 and 1970 (unit: ton)

	1961	*1970*
Hyogo	184,444	755,058
Kanagawa	302,707	622,868
Chiba	8,876	245,842
Okayama	113,855	221,175
Aichi	5,400	194,073
Shizuoka	105,176	162,206
Mie	44,438	149,705
Fukuoka	87,732	123,712
Total of top eight prefectures	852,628	2,474,639
Total in Japan	943,946	2,514,370

Source: Compiled by the author based on data from MAFF *The Situation of Oil-crop Industries* 1961, 1970.

Japan that year in factories operating in every prefecture. However, the volume of crushed domestic rapeseed decreased to 24,803 tons by 1970, that is, to less than a tenth of the amount at the beginning of the decade. Fourteen inland prefectures lost their oil production capacity completely. On the other hand, the volume of crushed imported rapeseed increased more than tenfold, from 33,491 tons in 1961 to 424,677 tons in 1970, with almost all of this rapid growth in prefectures with ports, including Hyogo (which has Kobe), Kanagawa (which has Yokohama), Fukuoka, Mie, Okayama, and Chiba. These data illustrate the structural shift in the rapeseed-crushing oil industry.

In the case of soy, the same dataset contains data on imported soy bean only, because, as we have seen, the Japanese soy-crushing industry depended on imported soy from the beginning. Table 4.7 shows the production volume from the top eight soy-crushing prefectures, which processed about 98% of imported soy by the beginning of the 1970s. They are all located in the so-called Pacific Belt industrial zone, the regions that contain the Japanese megalopolis and industrial areas clustered near the Pacific Ocean and the Seto Inland Sea.

In summary, these statistics demonstrate the intensification of oil-crop-crushing in larger factories in the port regions of Japan and the increased dependency of the oil businesses on imported crops as their main raw materials. The smaller factories inland, which had once crushed domestic rapeseed in almost every part of Japan, were effectively excluded from the industry in the course of a couple of decades.

This structural shift of the industry was further strengthened by national land planning and the modernization of the food industry.

The national planning of food industrial complexes

The Japanese government began discussing a radical reform of the food industry in the 1960s in order to prepare for the coming deregulation of trade and foreign investment. The Food Agency commissioned the Research Team to Reform and Rationalize the Food Industry (食品工業改善合理化研究会) to investigate how the Japanese food industry could become more efficient, so that they could face the incoming wave of imported food products and foreign food companies in the Japanese market. The Research Team set up a section to study the creation of a Japanese food industrial complex, which it called the "Food *Kombinat*." *Kombinat* is a Russian word; the USSR had built industrial *kombinat* into their planned economy since the 1920s. Japanese people had used the term to indicate the industrial complexes of Japan, mainly the petrochemical industry complexes that had been built in the Pacific Belt zone since the 1950s. When the Japanese government discussed the rationalization of the food industry, the same idea was adopted. In 1967, the Research Team provided its suggestions. In general, their report argued that the Japanese food industry consists of many inefficient, outdated small businesses; so rationalizing them into food *kombinats* would significantly reform the Japanese food industry, strengthening the competitive power of Japanese food companies in the global market and stabilizing the prices of commodities inside Japan (Food Industry Improvement and Rationalization Association 1967, 231).

More specifically, the Food *Kombinat* plan offered a three-step strategy to reform the structure of the Japanese food industry as bellow:

1 First, huge silos should be built in new or restructured ports so that imported commodities like wheat, soy beans, corn, and sugar could be easily discharged from large cargo vessels and stored in volume.
2 Then, first-stage food-processing factories in the *kombinat* should process these imported commodities into flour, vegetable oil, corn starch, and sugar to supply these basic food ingredients to the food-processing companies.
3 Finally, second-stage food-processing factories should use these ingredients to bake bread and manufacture products such as confections, soft drinks, and noodles. These processed food products should be distributed from huge distribution centers connected to the food *kombinat*.

The Ministry of Agriculture and Forestry and the major food companies collaborated to promote this Food *Kombinat* plan and asked for budget approval. It was discussed as part of the national planning of Japan.

The important point to notice here is that although the government discussed the overall reform of the Japanese food industry, the Food *Kombinat* plan focused on imported wheat, soy beans, maize, and sugar. Most of these are commodities from the United States, and they are mainly handled by large food companies. Many of the companies with such processing capacity were related to *zaibatsu* capital from the prewar era and *sogo-shosha* of the post-WWII era. YOSHIDA Tadashi, who studied post-WWII food integration, said that the Food *Kombinat* plan provided a playground for *sogo-shosha* to further strengthen their influence in the Japanese food industry and let huge capital clear away smaller food-processing companies (Yoshida 1971).

Discussion

The Japanese soy and oil industries that developed utilizing Manchurian soy and other oil crops in Asian regions were designated crucial wartime munitions manufacturers before and during WWII. After Japan was defeated in 1945, the same large companies shifted to using US soy and swiftly recovered their business as food companies supplying edible oils and food products to feed the starving nation.

Mass-produced soy oil and meal: Products and markets

Soy and other oil crops became important military materials as sources of bio-based oil and protein, serving as raw materials for a wide range of industries and military supplies to substitute for the lack of petroleum resources. The Japanese companies tried to manufacture lubricants, aviation oil, biofuels, explosives, and many other products out of Manchurian soy and other oil crops procured from the Asian regions that Japan occupied during the wars. Both the oil resources and the large oil and oleochemical companies were controlled by the military-government.

These companies that continued R&D and production for military purpose during WWII quickly pivoted to producing edible oil products to supply food markets in the defeated Japan. In the historical background of the lack of all commodities, the Japanese big companies who had oversized production capacity sought any raw materials to operate their factories. The concurrent US intention to export wheat and soy to overseas markets was greatly welcomed by these Japanese big business. It was a natural business strategy for the companies trying to fully utilize their production capacity and to adjust their products to the markets' needs; however, such historical and corporate reasons are seldom heard in the discussion of low self-sufficiency of food and oil crops in post-WWII Japan.

Soy and the "visible hands" of business and government

By the 1930s, the Japanese oil-related industries had formed an oligopoly of a few dominant companies. Then, as Japan moved deeper into wars in Asia and the Pacific, the Japanese military-government consolidated the oil and oleochemical industries as important war industries. While smaller companies were combed out for wartime efficiency and other civil manufacturers suffered from the lack of materials and human resources, the larger companies continued R&D and production under military orders during the war, utilizing resources from the Japanese occupation of Asian regions, including Manchukuo.

After WWII was over, these same oil companies utilized the technologies and production capacity they had developed during the war to quickly transform into food companies, which began supplying edible products to the Japanese food market. It is important to understand that the playing field was already not level when Japan began its post-WWII reconstruction, which left little room for smaller businesses or domestic agriculture. Although such dominant structure of the oil and oleochemical industries had been created for political and military reasons, it continued to benefit large corporations for peacetime food markets.

The role of soy in food and capitalist history: Incorporating Japan into the Second Food Regime

The modern Japanese oil-press and oleochemical industries had developed utilizing the rich oil crop and fish oil resources in Asia. The modernizing Japan had developed by extracting resources from these Asian territories as if a "core" country in the First Food Regime in the Asian context, as discussed in the earlier chapters. This structure was further strengthened when Japan went deeper in wars, and when it began using a slogan of "Greater East Asia Co-prosperity Sphere," that included Japanese-occupied China, Korea, Manchukuo, Southeast Asia, and some part of the Pacific. These occupied Asian territories allowed Japan to have access for the rich oil crops, including soy and rapeseed, among others, and these bio-based oils and proteins became essential resources for Japan, which lacked petroleum, to wage modern wars.

After the war, Japan came under US hegemony, not only in general socioeconomic structure but also in terms of food and oil crop resources and industries. US soy played a significant role to incorporate Japan into the overseas market for US agricultural products. One of the consequences was that Japanese companies and people were embedded in the Second Food Regime under US hegemony, as I discuss in Chapter 5.

Bibliography

In English

Clapp, J. (2012) *Hunger in the Balance: The New Politics of International Food Aid*, Cornell University Press.

Commonwealth Economic Committee (CEC 1948) *Vegetable Oils and Oilseeds: A Summary of Figures of Production, Trade and Consumption Relating to Groundnuts, Cottonseed, Linseed, Soya Beans, Coconut and Oil Palm Products, Olive Oil, and Other Oilseeds and Oils*, UK Stationery Office.

Friedmann, H. and McMichael, P. (1989) "Agriculture and the State System: The Rise and Decline of National Agricultures, 1870 to the Present", *Sociologia Ruralis*, 29(2), pp. 93–117.

Ito, A. (2021) "Japanese Market Development Programs under PL 480 in the late 1950s: Focus on Wheat and Rice", *Agricultural History*, 95(2), pp. 245–275.

Prodöhl, I. (2023). *Globalizing the Soybean: Fat, Feed, and Sometimes Food, c.1900–1950*, Routledge.

In Japanese (with English translation by the author)

Ajinomoto (1971) *The History of Ajinomoto (before WW2)* (味の素株式会社社史編纂室 [1971]『味の素株式会社社史 1』（戦前編）味の素).

Food Industry Improvement and Rationalization Association (1967) *Food Industry White Paper* (食品工業改善合理化研究会 [1967]『食品工業白書』全国食生活改善協会).

Hirano, S. (1973) *The Life Story of Yoshihara Sadajiro (Yoshihara Oil)* (平野成子[1973]『油ひとすじ: 吉原定次郎翁伝』吉原製油株式会社).

Honen Oil (1944) *The Corporate History 20 Years* (豊年製油[1944]『豊年製油株式會社二十年史』豊年製油).

Honen Oil (1963) *The Corporate History 40 Years* (豊年製油株式会社 [1963]『豊年製油株式会社四十年史』豊年製油).

Honen Oil (1993) *The Corporate History 70 Years* (ホーネンコーポレーション（豊年製油）[1993]『育もう未来を：ホーネン70年のあゆみ』).

Japan Oil News (1949) (日本油脂新報社『油脂年鑑』1949年版).

JFOA (Japan Fats & Oil Association) *soap industry (1972) *The History of Oil Industry* (日本油脂工業会 [1972]『油脂工業史』日本油脂工業会).

JOPA (Japan Oilseed Processors Association) *vegetable oil industry (1963) *A History of Japan Oilseed Processors Association* (油脂製造業会 [1963]『油脂製造業会小史』油脂製造業会).

JOPA (Japan Oilseed Processors Association) (1977) *The 15-Year History of Japan Oilseed Processors Association* (日本油脂協会 [1977]『日本油脂協会十五年史』日本油脂協会).

JOPA (Japan Oilseed Processors Association) (2012) *The 50 Years of Oil Industry and the Japan Oilseed Processors Association* (日本植物油協会・幸書房 [2012]『製油産業と日本植物油協会50年の歩み』日本植物油協会).

Kao Soap (1940) *The Corporate History 50 Years* (花王石鹸五十年史編纂委員会[1940]『花王石鹸五十年史』花王石鹸五十年史編纂委員会).

Kao Soap (1960) *The Corporate History 70 Years* (花王石鹸70年史編纂室 [1960]『花王石鹸七十年史』花王石鹸).
Kao Soap (1993) *The Corporate History 100 Years* (日本経営史研究所・花王株式会社社史編纂室編纂 [1993]『花王史100年（1890–1990）』花王).
Kubota, S. (1929) "On the Industry of Hardened-oil", *Journal of the Society of Chemical Industry, Japan* (久保田四郎 [1929]「硬化油工業に就て」『工業化学雑誌』32(4), pp. 392–398).
Kubota, S. (1937) "On the Industry of Glycerine", *Journal of the Society of Chemical Industry, Japan* (久保田四郎 [1937]「グリセリン工業に就て」『工業化学雑誌』40(5), pp. 372–379).
Murayama, T. (1941) *Oil Industry in the World and Japan's National Policy on Oil* (村山威士 [1941]『世界油脂工業の趨勢と我が油脂国策』工政会).
Nakajima, T. ed. (1967) *History of Industrial Development in Modern Japan: Food Industry* (中島常雄 編 [1967]『現代日本産業発達史 第18食品』現代日本産業発達史研究会).
Nishikawa, E. (1942) *The Control of Oil and Fat* (西川英三 [1942]『油脂統制の現状と将来: 本邦油脂統制の発展と目標』新経済社).
Nisshin Oil (1969) *The Corporate History 60 Years* (日清製油株式会社 [1969]『日清製油60年史』日清製油).
NOF (Nippon Oil & Fats Co.) (1967) *The Corporate History 30 Years* (日本油脂社史編纂委員会 [1967]『日本油脂三十年史』日本油脂株式会社).
Sekishita, M. (1987) *The US-Japan Trade Friction and Food Problems* (関下稔 [1987]『日米貿易摩擦と食糧問題』同文館出版).
Ueno, S. (1927) "The Outline of Japanese Hardened Oil Industry", *Journal of the Society of Chemical Industry*, (上野誠一 [1927]「硬化油工業の概要」『工業化学雑誌』30(12), pp. 878–882).
Yoshida, T. (1971) "Integration and Big Trading Company's Entry into Agriculture", in Ino, R., Teruoka, S., Shigetomi, K. (eds.), *The State Monopoly Capitalism and Agriculture* (吉田忠 [1971]「第4章第2節 インテグレーションと巨大商社の農業進出」、井野隆一・暉峻衆三・重富健一編『国家独占資本主義と農業』下巻、大月書店、pp. 386–424).

Statistics and Reports

Commonwealth Economic Committee, *Vegetable Oils and Oilseeds*, UK Stationery Office (1937–1973).
Food Agency *The Oil-Crop Statistics* (食糧庁業務第二部油脂課編 [1956]『油糧統計便覧: 含大豆食品・飼料』昭和31年、食糧庁).
Food Agency *The Oil-Crop Statistics Yearbook* (食糧庁 『油糧統計年報』1963, 1965, 1967, 1971).
MAFF (Ministry of Agriculture, Forestry and Fisheries (Japan), *The Situation of Oil-Crop Industries* (農林水産省食糧庁・食品流通局 『油糧工業の現況』), 1961, 1970, 1990–2001.
MAFF (Ministry of Agriculture, Forestry and Fisheries (Japan), *The Oil and Fat Situation of Japan* (農林水産省 『我が国の油脂事情』) 1974–2015.

Websites

Business Archives Online (丸善企業史料統合データベース; for business reports of related companies) https://j-dac.jp/bao, Japan Digital Archives Center.
FAOstat www.fao.org/faostat/, Food and Agriculture Organization of the United Nations.
Kobe University Digital Archive Newspaper Clippings Collection (神戸大学附属図書館 デジタルアーカイブ) www.lib.kobe-u.ac.jp/sinbun/, Kobe University.
MAFF *Food Balance Sheet* (農林水産省「食料需給表」) www.maff.go.jp/j/zyukyu/fbs/, Ministry of Agriculture, Forestry and Fisheries (Japan).
NDL Digital Collections (国立国会図書館デジタルコレクション) https://dl.ndl.go.jp/, National Diet Library (Japan).
USDA PSD Online www.fas.usda.gov/psdonline/, United States Department of Agriculture Foreign Agricultural Service (USA).

5 Increasing Japan's edible oil consumption (the post-WWII period of rapid economic growth)

Soy oil becomes an everyday foodstuff

Introduction

The surge in edible vegetable oil consumption in post-WWII Japan is generally explained as a consequence of increased demand as the Japanese diet became Westernized, or Americanized, along with their increasing incomes. Contrary to this widespread narrative, however, this chapter argues that the supply side actively encouraged the consumption of edible oils because the large oil-producing companies, who had developed in non-food industrial and military manufacturing until the end of WWII, now needed to expand their markets in food sectors to absorb their overproduction. The governments of both Japan and the United States supported these corporate efforts. This chapter investigates how the supply side promoted oil consumption with public relations campaigns to promote cooking with oil and eating oil-rich and fried foods. The development of food-processing industries, the introduction of fast-food restaurants and other food services, and the birth of supermarket chains together realized the mass-distribution of mass-produced oil-containing consumer goods. *Sogo-shosha*, or "general trading companies," played an important role in facilitating the structural integration of the processed food and livestock industries, which rely heavily on imported grains and oilseeds. In this way, vegetable oils became an everyday foodstuff in Japan.

The rapid increase in the edible oil supply in post-WWII Japan

Following WWII, Japan increased its imports of grains and oilseeds, including wheat, soy, rapeseed, and corn (maize), mainly from the United States. Previous research and the general discourse on diet change in post-WWII Japan tend to focus on the greater consumption of wheat and animal products (meat, eggs, and dairy), often blaming the so-called "American wheat strategy" (Takashima 1979; Suzuki 2003). In fact, the consumption of substantial amounts of oil and fat was driven by the new availability of

DOI: 10.4324/9781032678733-6

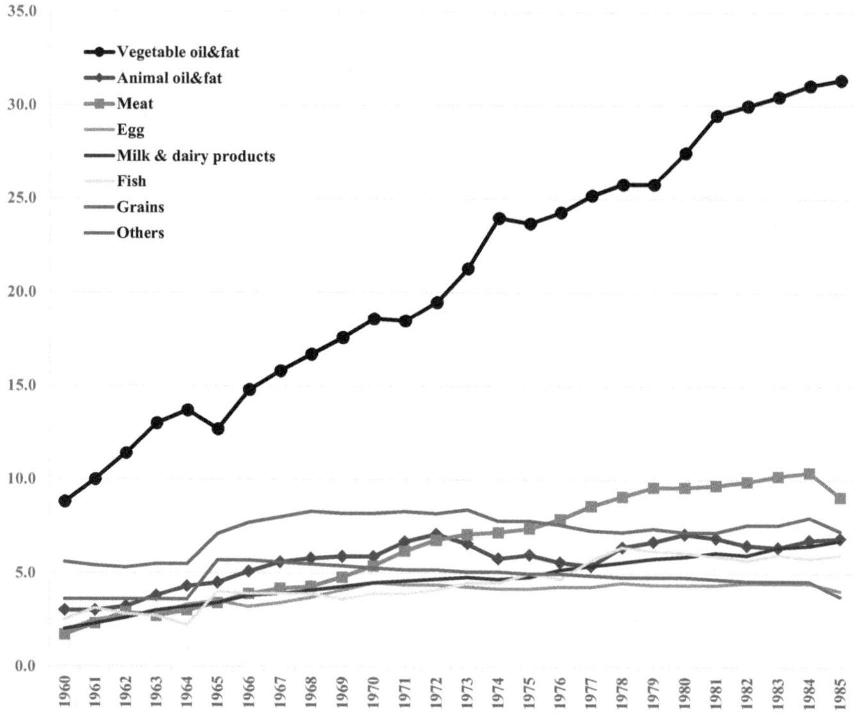

Figure 5.1 Daily per capita supply of fat (lipids) by food items in Japan, 1960–1985 (unit: gram).

Source: Produced by the author based on the data from the MAFF Food Balance Sheets.

vegetable oils, especially soy oil, rather than animal products (Figures 5.1 and 5.2). The political economy surrounding the significant growth in the supply and consumption of edible vegetable oils in Japan has been researched very little.

Accurate fat and oil consumption data are difficult to get, even today. Different kinds of oils and fats are easily mixed or substituted for each other, and end users pay less attention to what kind of oil they are using than to prices and availability. Nevertheless, the fragmented data that are available show that more oil and fat were used for industrial, military, and export purposes than for food in Japan until the end of WWII. The country's Food Agency recorded the average oil and fat consumption from 1934 to 1936 as 78,000 tons for food, 167,373 tons for non-food industries, and 98,435 tons for export (1956, 6). Another dataset shows the usage of vegetable oil consumed in 1945 as 9,560 tons for food, 106 tons for food industries,

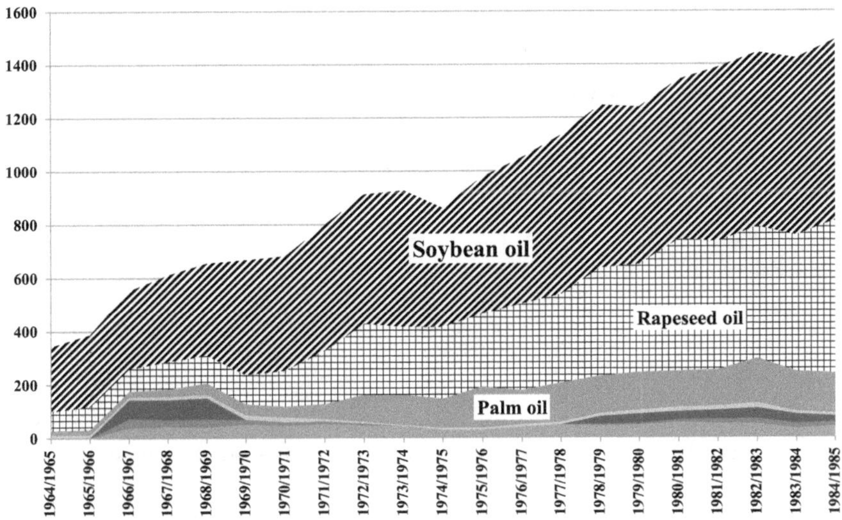

Figure 5.2 Domestic consumption of edible vegetable oils in Japan, 1964–1985 (unit: 1000 MT).

Source: Produced by the author based on the data from the USDA, Foreign Agricultural Service Production, Supply and Distribution.

13,068 tons for military supply, and 28,550 tons for liquid fuel (MAFF Oil Section 農林省油脂課, cited in Ooura and Hirano eds. 1948, 181). Thus, both contemporary records and corporate documents, as we saw in Chapter 4, indicate that much more vegetable oil was destined for non-food industrial uses, especially for military purposes and for export, until the end of WWII.

How, then, did the main usage of vegetable oils change in post-WWII Japan? Figure 5.3 shows the shift in the usage of soy oil and rapeseed oil, the main vegetable oils used in postwar Japan. The food use of these oils overtook the non-food use around 1955 and then continued to rapidly increase. What drove this change? The following sections reveal the political economic factors behind this sharp increase in the food consumption of vegetable oils in Japan.

Active campaigns to increase food-oil consumption

The US–Japan campaign to encourage wheat flour consumption among Japanese people in the post-WWII period is rather well known, both in academia and among the general public. The so-called "wheat strategy"

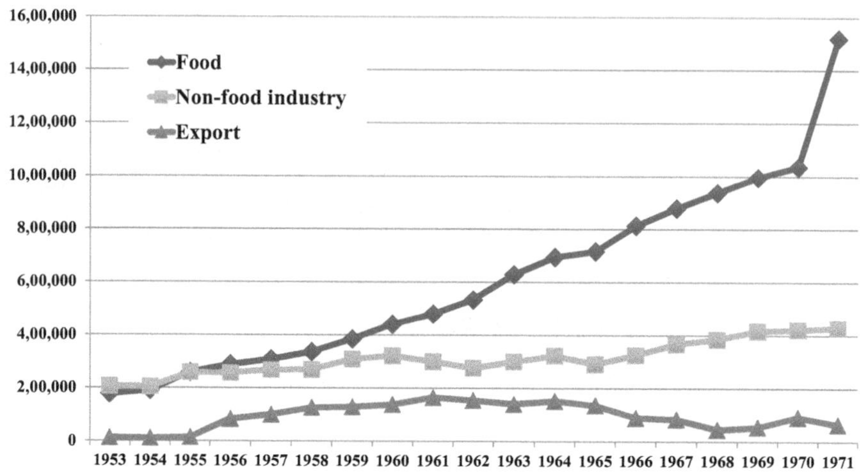

Figure 5.3 Shifting usage of soy oil and rapeseed oil in Japan, 1953–1971 (unit: crude oil ton).

Source: Produced by the author based on the data from Food Agency (1956, 1963) and MAFF (1971).

involved US food aid policy and urged the creation of overseas markets for America's surplus wheat production for the benefit of US farmers and grain traders. The Japanese Ministry of Health and Welfare collaborated in these projects, for example, with a campaign in which "kitchen cars" drove all around Japan, teaching new kinds of cuisine that used wheat flour and soy oil to Japanese housewives.

The active efforts to increase edible oil consumption, however, are little known, even in Japan. Even less known is that the Japanese themselves, led by their own government and businesses, took the initiative in promoting food products made mainly from imported US grains.

The "Eat More Oil" campaign since the 1950s

The Japanese oil companies took action as soon as the government ceased its control over the vegetable oil supply in 1950. The Tokyo Oil Wholesaler Market (東京油問屋市場) was revived, and it began active campaigns to increase edible oil consumption. From June to July 1951, the association organized a one-month "Tokyo Oil Festival" in the capital city, with a budget of over 5 million yen (the monetary value at the time). This event was supported by the Japanese government offices, including the Ministry of Agriculture and Forestry, the Food Agency, and the Tokyo Municipal government, as well as the industry association of the vegetable oil producers. The festival included a parade, a lottery with expensive cash prizes and goods, and many other events, all promoting the eating of more vegetable oils. Then, in March 1952, the association held a "Spring Oil Festival," inviting about 6,000 people to the Nichigeki Theater, the symbolic entertainment center of Japan.

Such festivals captured the attention of the Japanese public, but they were one-off events. For more continuous promotion, the Ministry of Agriculture and Forestry established the Oil and Fat Consumption Promotion Section in 1952 (油脂消費増進部会). This agency labeled the first week of September "Oil and Fat Week" every year from 1952 on. They then went from yearly to monthly reminders to eat more oils/fats by naming the first day of every month "Oil Day," beginning in 1956 (Tokyo Oil Wholesaler Market 2000).

Such active efforts indicate that Japanese companies were already producing too much vegetable oil. In those days, the major business magazine of the industry frequently discussed the overproduction of edible oils, for example, in articles that referred to the difficulty of selling rapeseed oil because of the oversupply of soy oil, which criticized companies that continued to import soy beans and extract oil from them. Around 1952, the price of soy fell and domestic rapeseed had a good harvest, and both the smaller and the larger oil companies, and both those that mainly crushed rapeseed and those that mainly crushed imported soy, sought to expand the domestic market of vegetable oils (Oil and Fat Monthly November 1952, 7–14).

The industry magazine featured interviews with SUGIYAMA Kintaro, the president of Honen Oil, at the beginning of 1953. In his view, the problem was that the domestic market for edible oils was too small, and he criticized government policies that promoted the increase in rapeseed production after the war without increasing the consumption of oil. He suggested that the country needed a "consumption increase movement." Furthermore, he continued, the movement should include oil producers, margarine and edible hardened oil manufacturers, oil and fat retailers, flour millers and breadmakers, the Japanese Federation of Economic Organizations (*Keidanren* 経団連), the Japan Chamber of Commerce and Industry, the Ministry of Agriculture and Forestry, the Ministry of Health and Welfare, the Ministry of Education, Science, Sports and Culture, and individuals and organizations in the fields of health and physical education, nutrition, schools, and media. In other words, the president of Honen Oil was calling for a national movement in which government, business, and civil sectors worked together to get people to eat more oil (Oil and Fat Monthly January 1953, 33).

The Nutrition Improvement and the "Frying-pan Movement"

As an effort to realize such a large-scale national movement, the Nutrition Improvement and Promotion Society (栄養改善普及会), which aimed to increase edible oil consumption in Japan, was established in March 1953. Although it claimed to be a voluntary civil organization, the Association had the ex-Minister of Health and Welfare as its president, and the heads of Honen Oil, Nisshin Flour Milling, and Meiji Dairies Corporation as vice presidents (Oil and Fat Monthly March 1953, 31).

The Association booklet explains how it started:

> We had gathered at the office of the Director of Public Health in the Ministry of Health and Welfare once a month since about three years before the foundation of the Association. Those who gathered there included the head of the New-Life Women's Association, a professor from Japan Women's University, a doctor from the National Institute of Nutrition, a staffer of the NHK, and officers of the Ministry. This group published a newsletter called "Bright Kitchens" (あかるい台所). We set up our office at Ms. Murakami's house, and we received the support of the executive members of Meiji Dairies Corporation, the Japan Dairy Products Association, and the Japan Margarine Industry Association. Based on this group, we founded the Nutrition Improvement and Promotion Society in March 1953, as an affiliated organization of the Ministry of Health and Welfare. Our core members included the industry associations of food companies, as well as the National Association of Housewives, the National Association of Local Housewives, and the Co-op, and we renamed our newsletter "Nutrition Improvement."
>
> (Nutrition Improvement and Promotion Society 1982, 6)

This organization was thus established with significant support from the companies that produced edible oils, wheat flour, dairy products, and margarine, and it was originally affiliated with the Ministry of Health and Welfare. KONDO Toshiko, who was a founding member and later led the movement as the chairperson of the Association, was an ex-officer in the Ministry of Health and Welfare. Later, their publication for the 30th anniversary of the movement included messages of praise from executive members of Nisshin Flour Milling Co., Meiji Dairies Corporation, Ajinomoto, and the Japanese Association of Soy Sauces, all of whom were vice presidents of the Association (Nutrition Improvement and Promotion Society 1982, 2–3). In short, the Nutrition Improvement and Promotion Society was well supported by big business and government.

The group that succeeded the Nutrition Improvement and Promotion Society is active to this day as a general incorporated association (www.fukyukai.jp). Its executive member list of 2017 included representatives from Nisshin Flour Milling Group, Nippon Flour Milling Co., Nisshin Oillio (Nisshin Oil) Group, J-Oil Mills (Honen Oil) Group, Showa Sangyo, Morinaga Dairy, and the Association of Japan Instant Food Industry Association.

Among its activities, the Society launched a nationwide "Frying-pan Movement" at the beginning of the 1960s, holding a "Frying-pan Movement assembly" in 1961, and organizing "traveling frying-pan cooking classes" in 1962. In 1963, an industrial association, the Japan Vegetable Oil Collaboration Association (JOPA),[1] formally asked the Nutrition Improvement and Promotion Society to conduct "a 'Let's Eat More Oil' campaign" and "a Frying-pan Movement for high school students" (JOPA 2012, 142). This campaign was co-organized by the Nutrition Improvement and Promotion Society, the Japan Vegetable Oil Collaboration Association, and the National Oil/Fat Retailers Association in collaboration with national organizations for home economics education (JOPA 2012, 146). This nationwide movement thus involved edible oil manufacturers, retailers, consumer groups, and the education sector.

The "Frying-pan Movement" targeted teachers of home economics and domestic science, housewives, mothers, the members of parent–teacher associations, the cooking staff of child welfare centers, and children. High school students were regarded as an important target for the movement. The Association encouraged students' research and activities to promote frying-pan cooking (using oil) or to popularize margarine (oil-containing processed food). They held a national assembly for the chosen high school student teams to present their activities, with a first prize presented by the Minister for Education. The Japanese–American Soybean Institute supported this movement for several years until 1966 (JOPA 1977). A photo of the 1961 "Assembly of the Once-a-Day Frying-pan Movement" shows a stage with a banner saying "Organized by the Nutrition Improvement and Promotion Society, The Japanese-American Soybean Institute" in their activity report (Nutrition Improvement and Promotion Society 1982).

Table 5.1 lists the Society's main activities for promoting edible oil and oil-related products from its foundation until the 1970s extracted from their publications.

As a part of their activities, a song was written to promote frying: the "Frying-pan Song" consists of four verses corresponding to the four seasons in Japan and cheerfully describing how "Mom" is always happy cooking with her frying pan. All four verses include the lyrics "with a frying-pan in her hand" and "use a frying-pan once a day" (Nutrition Improvement and Promotion Society 1961).

The Nutrition Improvement and Promotion Society identified itself as a consumer group and a women's movement, and they said their activities

Table 5.1 Events held by the Nutrition Improvement and Promotion Society, 1954–1977

Years	*Events*	*Notes*
1954	Fireless Cooking Presentation	Promoted meal preparation with canned food products, so that housewives can take day-off from cooking
1955	One-day housewife school	At the National Oil/Fat Retailers Association
1956	Housewife leaders held workshops	Held child nutrition classes for elementary school PTAs, New Year's guest-food classes, and oil cooking demonstrations at department stores
1958	Going out to promote cooking oils	Publicity by "wife lecturers" at department stores
	Classes on "bright" shopping	Recommending food products with oil and fats, bread, noodles, flour, margarine, fortified foods, etc.
1961	Once-a-Day margarine campaign; Once-a-Day Frying-pan Movement; recording of "Frying-pan Song"	
1962	Began the Mobile Frying-pan Cooking Class	Classes held for 26 times in Kyushu, Chugoku, Shikoku, Miyazaki, etc.
1963	High School Students Participated in Frying Movement Presentation for the First Time	Short performances of "Oil and I" and "Benefits of Oil"; the chorus of the "Frying-pan Song"
	Call for menus of frying-pan home dishes	
1964	High school students participated in Frying Movement presentation	Held every year since then
1965	In-store guidance by the Health teams	Voluntary dietary improvement activities formed in the previous year. They started giving in-store guidance at co-ops and agricultural cooperatives, such as "Let's eat oil more deliciously and correctly."
1967	Margarine promotion by high school students for the first time	
1968	Margarine promotion by high school students	Held every year since then
1969	"Price Survey" activities were particularly active	

Table 5.1 (Continued)

Years	*Events*	*Notes*
1970	"Soy Princess" from the American Soybean Association visited Japan	
1975	Appeal to the Ministry of Agriculture and Forestry and the Ministry of Health and Welfare to increase milk consumption	
1977	Promote "Rice, Oil, and Milk"	

Source: Compiled by the author based on data from Nutrition Improvement and Promotion Society (1982).

were supported by the volunteer work of many housewives (Nutrition Improvement and Promotion Society 1982, 1–3). In reality, however, their activity records suggest the involvement of government offices and food companies, especially in the wheat, edible oil, and dairy sectors. Under the name of "nutrition improvement," what the Association promoted most was food products made of wheat, soy, maize, and animal products—all commodities for which Japan heavily depended on imports, mainly from the United States. They recommended processed food products as "convenient," cheap, and high quality, and thus a help to housewives. Among the edible oils and oil products, what the "Frying-pan Movement" recommended was margarine rather than butter, corporate-refined soy oil rather than locally produced rapeseed oil, and commercially made mayonnaise rather than homemade mayonnaise.

Further research is needed to reveal how much and in what ways the government and the companies actually intervened in, or controlled, the activities of these "nutrition improvement" campaigns and/or the "Frying-pan Movement." It should also be remembered that the discourses of which foods or nutritional elements are good and which are bad do change over the decades. In those days, edible oil was recommended as "nutritious" because it provides more energy (with nine calories per gram) than rice (with four calories per gram). When many people had suffered starvation and malnutrition during and soon after the war, food items with higher calories could be considered "nutritious." It is important to consider discourses and general awareness of nutrition in those days before criticizing such campaigns for their specific nutritional recommendations. Still, it is clear that both the Japanese and US governments and the big oil and food businesses were actively involved in campaigns to promote the products that the Japanese food companies made, mostly based on imported US wheat, soy, maize, and sugar. This was part of the national movement that the president of Honen Oil aimed to organize to increase edible oil consumption in Japan to expand the markets for their products.

US–Japan joint PR campaign projects since the 1960s

The US government institutionalized more continuous, commercially based efforts than food aid to increase the export of US commodities through the Agricultural Trade Development and Assistance Act of 1954 (PL480). Soon afterward, in 1956, the Japanese–American Soybean Institute was established. This institute consisted of the American Soybean Association (ASA) and the Japanese soy-related companies in the fields of oil-refining and soy sauce, miso, and tofu manufacturing, and traders of these products. In 1965, ASA invited the first group of Japanese soy-related businessmen to the United States. Since its establishment, the Japanese–American Soybean Institute has taken the initiative in coordinating government and business activities in both the United States and Japan to actively promote the expansion of oil (thus soy) markets.

A strong Japanese counterpart was needed to deal with the US players; however, the Japanese oil industry in the 1960s was experiencing various internal conflicts: between the large and the small oil companies; between those who processed imported oil crops (mainly soy) and those who processed domestic oil crops (mainly rapeseed); and among oilseed crushers, oleochemical manufacturers, and retailers of oil/fat products over the allocation of raw materials or market shares. At the beginning of the 1960s, there were three main conflicting groups in the industry: The Japan Oilseed Processors Association; Honen Oil, the nation's largest oil company, which had left the Association; and the Japan Oil Crop Industry Cooperation Association, which was a group of the smaller oil companies.

The Japanese government was afraid that with all these conflicts in the Japanese oil industry, it would be difficult for the Japanese side to effectively collaborate with the US government and their soy-industry associations. So, the Minister of Agriculture and Forestry at the time summoned the presidents of ten major oil companies to demand that they unite the industry (JOPA 1977, 3–5). In response to this government instruction, the Japan Oil and Fat Association was founded in 1962, with SAKAGUCHI Yukio, the president of Nisshin Oil, as the head of the group. This association became the Japanese counterpart to the US side, which included the US Department of Agriculture, ASA, and other soy-related players. Together, they began the US–Japan Joint PR Project, which implemented large-scale PR campaigns to increase the consumption of edible oils in Japan to secure an overseas market for US soy.

The first stage of the US–Japan Joint PR Project was organized from November 1966 to June 1972 to promote oil/fat consumption in Japan, with a project budget of 120 million yen. Half of the project budget, 60 million yen, was paid by the US side, and the other half was paid by the Japanese oil companies, including Nisshin Oil, Ajinomoto, Honen Oil, Yoshihara Oil, Showa Sangyo, Japan Kyoyu, Nikka Oil, Linolic Oil, Fuji Oil, and Yokkaichi Oil. The American and Japanese sides also used the same project logo and slogan. In those days, the average daily per capita fat intake of Japanese people was a bit less than 20 grams. This amount was already a significant increase compared to the pre-WWII levels of less than 3 grams daily per capita, but the US–Japan Joint PR Project in the 1960s aspired to 30 grams. They held the campaign slogan of "Let's eat one meal a day cooked with vegetable oil." They conducted surveys, placed ads in magazines and newspapers, produced TV programs with cooking demonstrations, and held cooking classes to introduce cuisine using vegetable oil (mainly soy oil) to Japanese people (JOPA 1977, 77–86; JOPA 2012, 142–153).

Although statistics alone cannot prove the effects of this large-scale campaign, Japanese data show a significant fat intake increase in the middle of the 1960s, as illustrated in Figure 5.4. This post-WWII increase in oil/fat

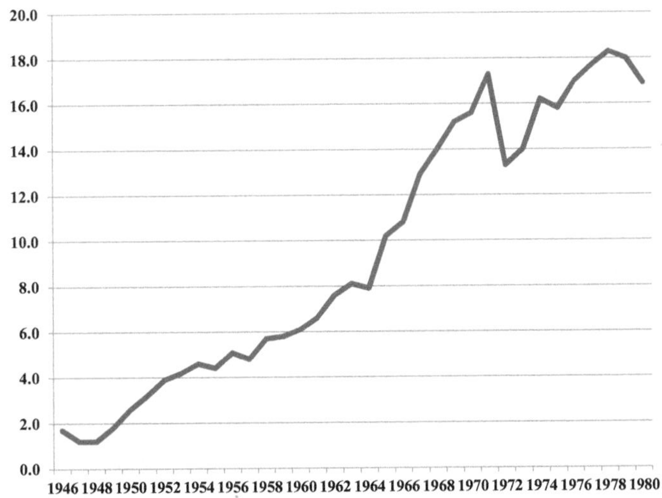

Figure 5.4 Post-WWII shift in daily per capita fat (lipids) intake by Japanese people (1946–1980) (unit: gram).

Source: Produced by the author based on the data from the National Health and Nutrition Survey by the Ministry of Health, Labour and Welfare.

consumption is often attributed to changing tastes and increasing incomes of consumers. Similar rhetoric is used to explain increasing soy imports in China and other emerging economies today. Still, the existence of the US–Japan Joint PR Project strongly suggest that well-funded, large-scale promotion by the government and big business influenced the demand for vegetable oils.

The structural increase in demand: Developing the food-processing and livestock industries

People do not drink edible oil out of the bottle or eat margarine by the spoonful. Thus, personal consumption at home was going to hit a peak sooner, rather than later, no matter how much capital governments and corporations invested in their "Eat More Oil" campaigns. The concurrent development of the processed food industries and the fast-food and other restaurant industries that use large amounts of oil as an ingredient or for cooking supported the increase in demand for grain and oilseeds. This section aims to reveal the structural increase in large-scale demand for soy and vegetable oils in post-WWII Japan by describing the development of the industries that manufacture margarine and shortening, instant noodles, and some other newly invented processed foods and snacks.

The development of margarine and shortening manufacturing

In the Western countries, margarine and shortening (aka "compound lard") gradually replaced the animal products of butter and lard. In the case of Japan, neither processed-oil nor animal products were commonly eaten before. It was only after WWII, especially from the middle of the 1950s, that the consumption of processed-oil products increased rapidly in Japan, about the same time that the country developed a full-scale modern livestock industry.

A small amount of margarine was being imported to Japan as early as 1887, and some Japanese entrepreneurs attempted to manufacture "artificial butter" by mixing and processing tallow, lard, soy oil, cottonseed oil, and/or peanut oil. These products largely remained at the trial stage before WWII (AJMA 1976, 184). In the case of shortening, it was a soap company, Kao Soap, that manufactured the first edible hardened oil product in Japan. Kao Soap had at one time imported coconut oil as a raw material to manufacture soap. They made the edible hardened oil product in 1928, naming it ECONA (Edible Coconut Oil of Nagase) (Nagase is the name of the founder of the Kao Soap company.) (AJMA 1976, 103; Kao Soap 1993, 109). Still, most hardened oil manufactured in Japan was used by the non-food and military supply industries (as discussed in Chapter 4), while only 4% of it was for edible purposes until the end of WWII (Kubota 1929).

When the production of margarine and shortening rapidly increased in the 1950s, the main buyers were industries rather than households. According to an industrial history, it took a long time for the use of margarine to disseminate into Japanese households; initially, "the bread industry and the Western confectionery industry were the large markets for the oil processors manufacturing margarine and shortening" (AJMA 1976, 218).

By the middle of the 1950s, however, Japan was already facing an oversupply of margarine and edible hardened oil products. By that time, the industry had been consolidated under the dominance of five large companies: Asahi Denka, Nippon Oil, Kanegafuchi Chemical, Miyoshi Oil, and Nikka Oil. In 1957, the top seven companies accounted for 51.1% of the margarine market, and they accounted for 55.3% of it by 1963 (AJMA 1976, 260, 283; Lion Oil 1979, 148). Many of these large companies were

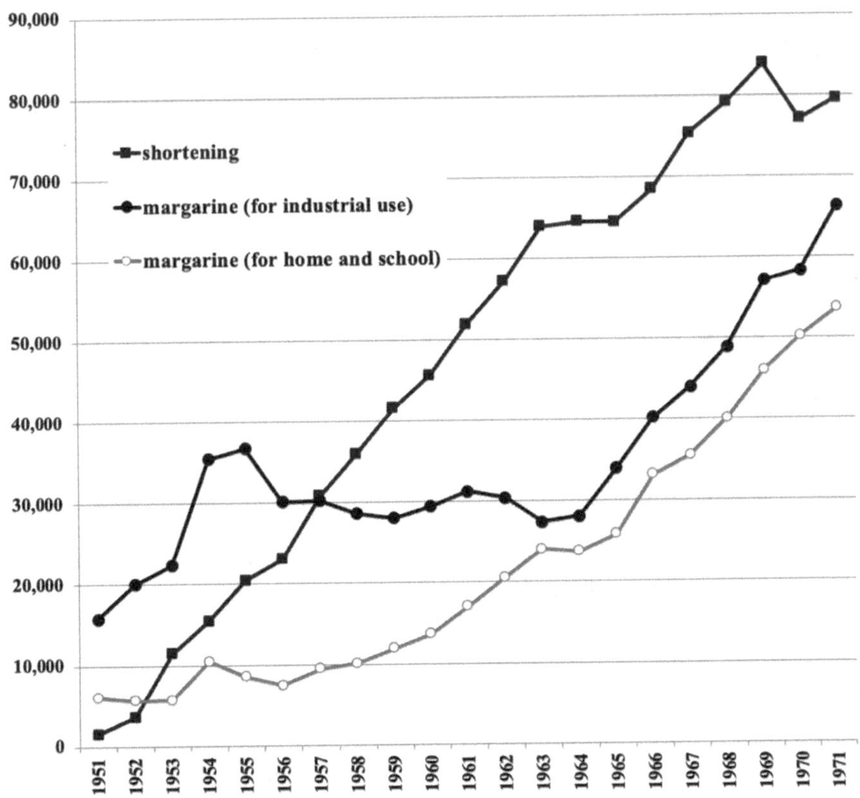

Figure 5.5 The production volume of margarine and shortening in Japan, 1951–1971 (unit: ton).

Source: Produced by the author based on the data from AJMA (1976, 322–323).

the same companies, or their successors, that had manufactured industrial and military oleochemical products during Japan's wars.

The birth of the instant noodle industry

Ramen was originally a Chinese noodle soup, but it became so popular in Japan that it is widely considered a Japanese food today. Although its Japanese history is rather short, ramen may have had a stronger effect on the popularization of a wheat flour diet among Japanese people than Western bread or cakes. As George Solt (2014) documented, soon after Yokohama port was opened in the latter half of the 19th century, the Chinese workers who lived there began making ramen noodles using the wheat flour and animal fats that Japan had just begun importing (Solt 2014). Ramen became popular among modern, urban, working-class people in Japan along with the country's industrial revolution and urbanization in the 1920s and 1930s. As Solt observed the spread of ramen, "a cheap, fast, and filling meal packed with salt, animal fat, and factory-processed wheat flour, fit neatly within the structure of modern industrial life" (2014, 5–6).

Soon after WWII, when the Ministry of Health and Welfare was struggling to popularize the wheat flour diet among Japanese in order to increase the market for US wheat, ANDO Momofuku, the founder of Nissin Food, recommended noodles as better suited to Japanese people than bread. This is a known episode in the birth of the instant noodle. Ando was a businessman, and he thought the obstacle to noodles' greater popularity was that individuals or tiny family businesses made them; he suggested that what was needed was to scale up noodle manufacturing into a mechanical-industry so that it could process larger volumes of US wheat to mass-produce ramen, which could then be mass-distributed to Japanese people (Ando 1983, 120–121). Ando invented a method to deep-fry noodles, making them porous, so they would soften quickly after hot water was poured onto them. In this way, the noodles became a processed food product that could be mass-produced in factories, and the noodle industry became a large buyer of wheat flour and frying oil. Nissin Food's first instant noodle product, Chicken Ramen, went on the market in 1958.

Ando argued that several conditions in 1950s Japan made it possible to mass-produce and mass-distribute instant noodle products. First, the government relaxed its control over the wheat and wheat flour trade in 1952, so it became easier for private companies to buy and sell wheat, flour, and wheat-flour-based products. Second, the first supermarket chains emerged in 1958, a revolutionary development in Japanese retail systems that made the nationwide mass-distribution of instant noodles and other processed foods possible. Third, more Japanese households had obtained television sets, and TV commercials became available as a strong advertising tool to promote new food products. In fact, Nissin Food actively utilized this new PR tool by becoming a sponsor of TV programs and running many commercials for chicken ramen and their other products (Ando 1983, 143–144).

The production of instant noodles increased rapidly, from 13 million packages in 1958 to 5 billion packages in 1990. Although actual data on how much frying oil has been used, or which oil or fat has been used for frying, to manufacture instant noodles are not publicly available, it seems clear that the instant noodle industry has had a part in the significant increase in the demand for oil and fat, as well as wheat flour, in Japan.

The dissemination of oil-rich cooking and eating practices through the development of processed food products

The invention of instant noodles kickstarted a new era of instant food products. Around the same time, in the 1950s, a wide range of other new factory-made processed foods arrived in the Japanese market. Table 5.2 lists

Table 5.2 Some of the new, oil-rich food products sold in post-WWII Japan, 1949–1972

	New food products
1949	Meiji Caramel
1950	Potato Chips
1952	Fujiya Milky
1954	Snow Brand Neo Soft Margarine
1955	Mama Spaghetti (Nisshin Seifun)
1958	**Chicken Ramen (Nissin Foods),** Almond Chocolate (Glico)
1960	House Indo Curry, Instant Coffee
1961	Creep (Morinaga Milk Industry), Marble Chocolate (Meiji), Instant ramen noodles with soup
1962	Marushin Hamburger Steak, Meisei Ramen
1963	Vermont Curry (House Foods), Pretz (Glico) Corn Flakes (Kellogg's), Knorr Soup (Ajinomoto)
1964	Kappa Ebisen (Calbee)
1965	**Retortable food products**
1966	Pocky (Glico)
1967	Sea Chicken (Harokoro Foods), Ebara Yakiniku sauce, many frozen foods
1968	Bon Curry and Bon Stew (Otsuka), Ajinomoto Mayonnaise
1969	UCC Canned Coffee
1970	Ajinomoto Marina margarine
1971	Cup Noodle (Nissin Foods), Lady Bowden (Meiji Dairies)
1972	Seasoning for mapo-tofu (Sichuan style bean curd), many frozen food products, many snack food products

Source: Adapted by the author, extracting oil-rich new products, from Kozuka (1999, 232–233).

Note: Bold letters are emphasis by the author.

some of these new processed foods and snacks, many of which, like potato chips and Kappa Ebisen, used wheat flour and oil/fat. In addition to ready-to-eat prepared foods, several other new food products to be used in home cooking impacted the daily home eating of Japanese people. For instance, various salad dressing products popularized the eating of raw salads. A canned meat pasta sauce was launched in 1959, a solid curry roux in 1960, and a Chinese mapo tofu seasoning became available in 1966. These new products of seasonings or mixes were marketed as helping Japanese housewives cook new kinds of cuisine at home, and it has been said that such products contributed significantly to popularizing the cooking of foreign dishes in Japanese households in the 1960s (Iwamura 2010, 130–134). While cooking such dishes at home, of course, Japanese consumers increased their oil consumption.

Kitchen facilities changed to encourage oil-rich cooking at home, too. The Japan Housing Corporation, a public corporation that has mass-built residences for urban workers since the middle of the 1950s, provided kitchens with gas cooking stoves and exhaust fans to allow deep-frying at home (Kozuka 1999, 160).

The rapid growth of the restaurant industry and the habit of eating out

Processed food and instant food products were part of the era of mass-production and mass-consumption that arrived in Japan in the 1960s and 1970s. Many standardized products were mass-produced in factories, and they were distributed via the supermarkets that emerged concurrently. Then, fast-food chains and other restaurant businesses developed since the beginning of the 1970s. The habit of eating out became normal, and the restaurants further popularized new dishes with lots of oil/fat and animal products. In Japan, immediately after the war, the restaurant business was strictly limited, partly because of the severe lack of food in Japan. Only designated restaurants, hotels, and cafes could serve food, although food services operated illegally in the black market. Even after the Japanese economy overcame the shortage of food, and the restrictions on restaurant businesses were repealed, eating out was reserved for very special occasions for the majority of Japanese people. Then, a change in government policy welcomed foreign capital investment in food sectors. Foreign capital investment had been deregulated gradually, until 100% foreign investment in restaurant businesses became possible in 1969. Foreign (mostly American) fast-food chains rushed into the Japanese market beginning in 1970, which is called "the first year of eating out" in Japan. Kentucky Fried Chicken (KFC) came in 1970; McDonalds, Mister Donut, and Dunkin Donuts in 1971; Dairy Queen in 1972; Pizza Hut in 1973; and Shakey's Pizza in 1974, to give a few examples (Kozuka 1999, 218). In many cases, the foreign capital coming into Japan worked with *sogo-shosha* as their partners on the Japanese side. In the case of the fast-food chains, for instance, Mitsubishi Corporation worked with KFC and Shakey's Pizza, Sumitomo Corporation with Pizza Hut, and Marubeni with Dairy Queen (Kozuka 1999, 218–220). McDonalds took on a Japanese businessman, FUJITA Den and his company, as a partner.

In summary, Japanese people increased their oil and fat intake by multiple routes. The development of food-processing industries and restaurant services that used large amounts of oil as an ingredient or for cooking, and of mass-distribution systems for processed food, led to a rapid increase in the supply of many kinds of oil-rich food products in the Japanese domestic market, including breads, snacks, fast foods, and instant noodles. In addition, the newly available seasoning and mix products popularized oil-rich cooking at home, and Japanese housewives began cooking dishes such as curry, stew, spaghetti, and mapo tofu for the family dinner at home, as well as deep-frying some foods. Soon, eating out also became a casual, daily activity for many Japanese people, and many of the fast-food and other restaurants use large amounts of oil and fat, as well as dairy and meat products.

This structural change in the food industries of mass-production and the revolution in retail systems of mass-distribution of products, as well as the development of TV commercials and many other marketing methods, were behind the surging demand for edible oil in post-WWII Japan.

The increased demand for soy meal as animal feed

As we have seen, soy meal for fertilizer was once the main product of the Japanese soy oil industry. Then, this protein-rich product became a raw material for industrial and military manufacturing during the wars, as well as for MSG. In post-WWII Japan, the major use of soy meal became animal feed to support the modern large-scale livestock industry that was introduced to Japan mainly from the United States.

Table 5.3 shows the shift in the usage of soy meal in Japan from the end of the 1950s to the beginning of the 1970s. Some amount of soy meal continued to be used for making food products, including miso, soy sauce, and MSG, but those usages stayed level or decreased, while the usage of soy meal for fertilizer and feed rapidly increased. This dataset includes fertilizer and feed in one category, but because most farmers were using chemical fertilizers by then, the growth it shows is primarily reflects an increase in soy meal used for animal feed.

Table 5.3 The volume of soy meal consumption in Japan according to use, 1958–1971 (unit: tons)

	1958	*1959*	*1960*	*1961*	*1962*	*1963*	*1964*
Miso	64,000	52,300	53,000	26,000	21,000	19,000	15,000
Soy sauce	150,000	153,800	155,000	151,000	148,000	158,000	165,000
Tofu, fried tofu	12,000	20,000	20,000	30,000	30,000	65,000	64,000
MSG	58,000	64,800	64,000	60,000	42,000	7,000	0
Other	5,000	30,000	30,000	30,000	50,000	68,000	43,000
Total food use	289,000	320,900	322,000	297,000	291,000	317,000	287,000
Chemical manufacturing	14,000	14,800	13,000	12,000	11,000	0	0
Feed and fertilizer	226,000	281,000	304,000	366,000	431,000	**612,000**	**698,000**
Export	4,000	4,300	2,000				5
Other							
Total non-food use	244,000	300,100	319,000	67,500	442,000	612,000	698,005
	1965	*1966*	*1967*	*1968*	*1969*	*1970*	*1971*
Miso	13,000	10,000	10,000	7,000	5,000	10,000	10,000
Soy sauce	170,000	162,000	171,000	160,000	154,000	168,000	170,000
Tofu, fried tofu	77,000	77,000	70,000	78,000	78,000	78,000	78,000
MSG	0	0	n.d.	n.d.	n.d.	n.d.	n.d.
Other	43,000	43,000	44,000	53,000	52,000	57,000	60,000
Total food use	303,000	292,000	295,000	298,000	289,000	313,000	318,000
Chemical manufacturing	5,000	5,000	5,000	5,000	4,000	3,000	3,000
Feed and fertilizer	**818,000**	**964,000**	**952,000**	**1,074,000**	**1,281,000**	**1,631,000**	**1,784,000**
Export	5,000	3,000	3,000	2,000	3,000	0	0
Other			5,000	5,000	5,000	8,000	8,000
Total non-food use	828,000	972,000	965,000	1,086,000	1,293,000	1,642,000	1,795,000

Source: Compiled by the author based on the data from the Food Agency *The Oil-Crop Statistics Yearbook* of 1963, 1967, 1971.

Note: Bold values are emphasis by the author.

Sogo-shosha: Integrating the food and livestock industries

The fast-food sector developed as a part of the integration of the food and livestock industries that the *sogo-shosha* had invested in. For example, Mitsubishi Corporation, which invested in KFC Japan, also had shares in grain-importing, feed-manufacturing, and broiler- and meat-packing businesses. Such "food integration" or "livestock integration" is the significant contributor of the oil-rich and meaty diet in the Japanese food system, in which the corporate groups import grains; process them at the Food *Kombinat* in the port regions into wheat flour, vegetable oil, sugar, and feed; supply these ingredients to large-scale food-processing and livestock companies; and mass-distribute the products to the supermarket chain retailers and the fast-food chains and other restaurants, which they also own. The *sogo-shosha* played significant roles in these processes of integration.

The Japanese traders reestablished as sogo-shosha

The Japanese *zaibatsu*, who had collaborated with the Japanese government to modernize the country since the 19th century, was dissolved by the order of the Supreme Commander for the Allied Powers (SCAP) when Japan was defeated in 1945. Mitsui and Mitsubishi were broken down into hundreds of small businesses each, for example, and the *zaibatsu* officially disappeared. International trade was controlled by the government for defeated Japan, and public corporations were built in 1947 to handle actual trading operations in the fields of minerals, textiles, food, and industrial raw materials (Japan Trade Research Association 1967, 525–527).

While the previously dominant *zaibatsu*-traders were being broken apart and weakened, some traders from Western Japan (the Kansai area) became stronger. They included traders linked to today's Marubeni, Itochu, and Sojitz. They originated in Western Japan, Omi region (today's Shiga prefecture) or Kobe, and had been strong in the fields of textiles or iron and steel until the end of WWII. Marubeni and Itochu originated from the same Ito family, who had been traders in the Omi area since the Edo period. Sojitz is the successor of Nissho-Iwai, which originated from Suzuki Shoten (Tsuji 1992, 77–109; Nissho 1968). After WWII, although the SCAP ordered them to limit their activities, Marubeni and Itochu managed to survive by reshaping their corporate bodies and other methods. The trading conditions immediately after the defeat gave them an advantage, because Japan's main trade until around 1950 was importing raw textile materials, food, and machines, and exporting textile products. The restricted trading conditions under government control encouraged these companies to widen the range of trade items they handled beyond textiles or iron/steel, and they thus became "general" trading companies (Oomori 2011, 164–169). Today, both Marubeni and Itochu are quite active in grain trading and other food industries inside and outside Japan (Tsuji 1992, 11–76; Marubeni 1977).

International trade was gradually deregulated, and the Korean War (1950–1953) boosted business for these traders. The Japanese government wanted the Japanese traders to become stronger, and so the government supported them (Tsuji 1992, 38–39). In this context, the ex-*zaibatsu* traders also reassembled; Mitsubishi Corporation restarted in 1954, and Mitsui&Co. in 1959 (Oomori 2011, 169–171).

In this way, Mitsubishi, Mitsui, Marubeni, Itochu, and some other traders had transformed into general trading companies (*sogo-shosha*) by the middle of the 1950s, about when the Japanese economy entered its period of rapid and intensive economic growth. The *sogo-shosha* began entering the food and livestock sectors more actively, as the food and livestock industries became bigger business, and as the international trade of food and agricultural products became more deregulated.

Integrating the food and livestock industries

During Japan's period of intensive economic growth from 1955 to the early 1970s, the *sogo-shosha* actively entered agriculture, especially in the livestock industry. The Integration Research Group, which has studied these phenomena, said that *sogo-shosha* integrated segments of the Japanese food systems, both vertically from production to distribution to retail and restaurant services, and horizontally in more than one product at the same stage (Miyazaki 1972, 36–37).

In previous research on agricultural integration in Japan, MIYAZAKI Hiroshi outlined the stages of *sogo-shosha* integration in livestock industries as below:

Step 1: Contract farming with *shosha* capital (from war-end until 1960)
Around the middle of the 1950s, American-style contract farming for broiler chickens, in which large capital provides chicks and feed to the farmers and buys up all the grown chickens, was introduced to Japan. One of the first such systems was established between chicken dealers in Tokyo and farmers in Gunma Prefecture.

Step 2: Integration around feed companies (1960–1963)
Sogo-shosha that imported grains and had feed companies in their group began to expand to broiler chicken businesses connected to their feed companies. They faced competition with the traditional chicken traders and the agricultural cooperatives in Japan, but the *sogo-shosha* had stronger control over feed and chicks, and they had more capital. The *sogo-shosha* actively encouraged the modern large-scale livestock industries of broiler chicken and pig farming.

Step 3: The establishment of *sogo-shosha* integration (1964–1968)
Against the background of Japan joining the International Monetary Fund and the General Agreement on Tariffs and Trade in the 1950s, and deregulating investment and the movement of capital in the 1960s, the *sogo-shosha* began to actively invest in the food and agricultural sectors in 1964.

Step 4: Direct investment in farms (1968–1970s)
In addition to expanding contract farming, some *sogo-shosha*, including Mitsubishi, Itochu, Sumitomo, and Nissho-Iwai (later Sojitz), began directly investing in farms.

Step 5: The development of the Food *Kombinat*
As the petrochemical heavy industries concentrated in the Pacific Belt zone, the government encouraged the large-scale food companies to gather there as the Food *Kombinat* (see Chapter 4). The *sogo-shosha* handled the import of grains to Japan and also had invested in many of the first food processors (flour-milling, oilseed-crushing, sugar-manufacturing, etc.) and some other food-processing businesses. They now began taking the so-called "develop and import" approach, in which Japanese capital goes overseas to develop agricultural crop production for import to Japan (extracted from Miyazaki 1972, 53–63).

The *sogo-shosha* did not single-handedly establish this integration in the food and livestock industry, of course. Still, they have been significant actors in forming a major part of the Japanese food system, from the import of grains, through the first-stage processing—flour-milling, oil-refining, sugar-manufacturing, and feed-manufacturing—and on to the second-stage food-processing that uses these ingredients (i.e., wheat flour, vegetable oil, sugar, and animal products) and the livestock-raising that uses the feed. They have also been involved in food distribution, retailing, and fast-food/restaurant businesses. Soy and vegetable oils, the focus of this book, are deeply embedded in these food and livestock integration structures.

Discussion

Even before Japan's high economic growth began in the middle of the 1950s, the supply of vegetable oils had surpassed the domestic food demand. Therefore, the supply side, which includes both the Japanese and US governments and big business, actively promoted the increase in edible soy oil and soy meal consumption, through conducting PR campaigns to reach individual consumers as well as engineering the structural increase in large-volume demand by developing the processed food industries, fast-food and other restaurant industries, and livestock industries.

Mass-produced soy oil and meal: Products and markets

The edible uses of soy oil and rapeseed oil, the major vegetable oils in Japan after WWII, surpassed the non-food industrial usages in the 1950s, and vegetable oils became cheap and abundant basic foodstuffs in Japan for the first time. The "Eat More Oil" campaign and "Frying-pan Movement," which were funded and promoted by big business and governments, disseminated the practice of using cooking oils in Japanese households. The new processed food products like potato chips and instant noodles, many of which were made with imported grains and oilseeds, increased Japanese peoples' fat intake via factory-made products. A wide range of many new processed food products arrived on the market, and these mass-produced food products were mass-distributed by the newly developed supermarket system. With the deregulation of the restaurant and fast-food industries, which also center on oil-rich foods, eating out came to be a daily, or at least an ordinary, event. Concurrently, the livestock industries based on soy meal as feed input grew rapidly, thus increasing the supply of meat and dairy products as well as the demand for soy meal. In this way, both the supply and consumption of soy oil and meal increased significantly in post-WWII Japan as a part of the mass-production and mass-consumption era.

Soy and the "visible hands" of business and government

Consumer demand for oily food and animal food products because of economic growth and the Westernization of diets is often given as the explanation for increased soy imports. This chapter, however, demonstrated that the supply of vegetable oils exceeded demand already in the first half of the 1950s, before Japan entered its period of high economic growth. The Japanese oil industries, and the Japanese and US governments, their soy associations, and the large companies involved in oil, wheat, milk, feed, and livestock, together conducted PR campaigns aiming to increase the consumption of oily food and animal products among Japanese people. In addition to such campaigning efforts to increase the demand from individual consumers, large-scale institutional demand also increased through the development of the food-processing, food service, and livestock industries. The birth of instant noodles, for example, realized the mass-production of factory-made noodle products, which required the mass-consumption of wheat flour and frying oils, and was built on grain and oilseed imports, mainly from North America. The governments of Japan and the United States supported and encouraged this move for their own reasons.

The role of soy in food and capitalist history: The Japanese side integrating into the US-centered agri-food complexes

The previous literature on the increase in wheat and soy imports of post-WWII Japan tends to blame the United States' strategies to increase its overseas markets for their agricultural crops, like the "American wheat strategy." As this chapter has demonstrated, however, this shift in consumption trends was led by both the Japanese and United States governments and big businesses. The Japanese government and the large Japanese companies in soy, oil, wheat, and trading, which had established dominance by the end of WWII, actively "copied" US models and "integrated" themselves into the soy-corn-animal complex and the durable (processed) food complex under US hegemony in the Second Food Regime (Friedmann and McMichael 1989). It was a part of Japanese strategy to develop themselves in the world-economy.

Note

1 The industry association, that mainly handled oil crops and vegetable oils, has changed its Japanese names from Japan Oilseed Processors Association (油脂製造業会) to the Japan Oil and Fat Association (日本油脂協会), then to the Japan Vegetable Oil Association (日本植物油協会); however, they have used the same English name and the abbreviation JOPA. This book uses this English name and abbreviation for the reference information.

Bibliography

In English

Friedmann, H. and McMichael, P. (1989) "Agriculture and the State System : The Rise and Decline of National Agricultures, 1870 to the Present", *Sociologia Ruralis*, 29(2), pp. 93–117.

Solt, G. (2014) *The Untold History of Ramen: How Political Crisis in Japan Spawned a Global Food Craze*, University of California Press.

In Japanese (with English translation by the author)

All Japan Margarine Association (AJMA) (1976) *The History of Japanese Margarine Industry* (全日本マーガリン協会 [1976]『日本マーガリン工業史』幸書房).

Ando, M. (1983) *Outrageous Ideas*, (安藤百福 [1983]『奇想天外の発想』講談社).

Iwamura, N. (2010) *The Comedy on the Table Shown with 274 Photos* (岩村暢子 [2010]『家族の勝手でしょ!: 写真274枚で見る食卓の喜劇』新潮社).

Japan Trade Research Association (1967) *The 20 Year History of Trade in Post-War Japan* (日本貿易研究会 [1967]『戦後日本の貿易20年史: 日本貿易の発展と変貌』通商産業調査会).

JOPA (Japan Oilseed Processors Association) (1963) *A History of Japan Oilseed Processors Association* (油脂製造業会 [1963]『油脂製造業会小史』油脂製造業会).

JOPA (Japan Oilseed Processors Association) (1977) *The 15-Year History of Japan Oil and Fat Association* (日本油脂協会 [1977]『日本油脂協会十五年史』日本油脂協会).

JOPA (Japan Oilseed Processors Association) (2012) *The 50-Year of Oil Industry and Japan Vegetable Oil Association* (日本植物油協会・幸書房 [2012]『製油産業と日本植物油協会50年の歩み』日本植物油協会).

Kao Soap (1993) *The Corporate History of Kao 100 Years* (日本経営史研究所・花王株式会社社史編纂室編纂 [1993]『花王史100年（1890–1990）』花王).

Kozuka, Y. (1999) *Diet Change and the Growth of Food Manufacturers* (小塚善文 [1999]『食の変化と食品メーカーの成長』農林統計協会).

Kubota, S. (1929) "On the Industry of Hardened-Oil", *Journal of the Society of Chemical Industry, Japan* (久保田四郎 [1929]「硬化油工業に就て」『工業化学雑誌』32(4), pp. 392–398).

Lion Oil (1979) *The Corporate History of Lion 60 Years* (ライオン油脂株式会社社史編纂委員会編集 [1979]『ライオン油脂六十年史』ライオン油脂株式会社).

Marubeni (1977) *The Early History of Marubeni* (丸紅株式会社 [1977]『丸紅前史』丸紅).

Miyazaki, H. (1972) *Agricultural Integrations* (宮崎宏 [1972]『農業インテグレーション』家の光協会).

Nissho (1968) *The 40-Year History of Nissho*, (日商株式会社 [1968]『日商四十年の歩み』日商).

Nutrition Improvement and Promotion Society (1961) *Once a Day Frying-pan Movement Activity Report* (栄養改善普及会 [1961]『1日1回フライパン運動1961』（資料 No.42 活動報告書）.

Nutrition Improvement and Promotion Society (1982) *Thirty Years of Walking and Thinking*, (栄養改善普及会 [1982]『歩きながら考える三十年』栄養改善普及会出版).

Oomori, K. (2011) "Restructuring of *sogo-shosha* in Post-War Japan", in Oomori, K., Ooshima, H., and Kiyama, M. (eds.), *The History of sogo-shosha*. (大森一宏 [2011]「戦後総合商社の再編」、大森一宏・大島久幸・木山実編著『総合商社の歴史』関西学院大学出版会、pp. 163–173).

Ooura, M. and Hirano, S. eds. (1948) *Golden Flower: The History of Japan Oil Company* (大浦万吉・平野茂之 編 [1948]『黄金の花: 日本製油株式会社沿革史（改訂増補版）』新潮社).

Suzuki, T. (2003) *The US Wheat Strategy* (鈴木猛夫 [2003]『「アメリカ小麦戦略」と日本人の食生活』藤原書店).

Takashima, T. (1979) *The US Wheat Strategy* (高嶋光雪 [1979]『アメリカ小麦戦略：日本侵攻』家の光協会).

Tokyo Oil Wholesaler Market (2000) *The History of Tokyo Oil Wholesalers* (東京油問屋市場 [2000]『東京油問屋史：油商のルーツを訪ねる』東京油問屋市場).

Tsuji, S. (1992) *A Study on Kansai sogo-shosha: How They Became General Trading Companies*, (辻節雄 [1992]『関西系総合商社: 総合商社化過程の研究』晃洋書房).

Statistics and Reports

Food Agency *The Oil-Crop Statistics Yearbook* (食糧庁 『油糧統計年報』).
MAFF (Ministry of Agriculture, Forestry and Fisheries (Japan) *The Oil and Fat Situation of Japan* (農林水産省 『我が国の油脂事情』).

Websites

Business Archives Online by (丸善企業史料統合データベース; for business reports of related companies) https://j-dac.jp/bao, Japan Digital Archives Center.
FAOstat www.fao.org/faostat/, Food and Agriculture Organization of the United Nations.
Kobe University Digital Archive Newspaper Clippings Collection (神戸大学附属図書館 デジタルアーカイブ) www.lib.kobe-u.ac.jp/sinbun/, Kobe University.
MAFF *Food Balance Sheet* (農林水産省「食料需給表」) www.maff.go.jp/j/zyukyu/fbs/, Ministry of Agriculture, Forestry and Fisheries (Japan).
MHLW National Health and Nutrition Examination Survey www.mhlw.go.jp/bunya/kenkou/kenkou_eiyou_chousa.html, Ministry of Health, Labour and Welfare (Japan).
Oil and Fat Monthly Magazine (1952, 1953), published by Saiwai Shobo, www.saiwaishobo.co.jp/monthly-yushi/, Saiwai Shobo.
USDA PSD Online www.fas.usda.gov/psdonline/, United States Department of Agriculture Foreign Agricultural Service.

Conclusion

Soy and capitalist development

Japan began importing Manchurian soy in the 19th century, and the Japanese government, colonial institutions, and big business invested heavily in the development of the soy-industry and the global trade of soy bean, meal, and oil. These actors established large-scale, capital-intensive, mechanical-industrial mass-production and mass-distribution structures for soy products *before* the Japanese diet demanded such products. Instead, the soy-industry needed to pour significant efforts into research and development, expanding the versatility of soy in order to find new markets for the mass-sale of their mass-produced soy oil and meal. The same actors, along with the US government and American soy interests, were also behind the public relations campaigns that disseminated the practices of deep-frying and oil-rich cooking at home and in restaurants in post-WWII Japan, and propagated the "Westernization" of the Japanese diet to build domestic demand for oils/fats and animal products. This contradicts a common belief about food and agriculture, according to which economies import more grain and oilseeds when local consumers demand more oils/fats and animal products due to economic development and increasing incomes.

This book demonstrated how the soy-industry developed to include industrial large-scale agriculture to produce soy as a raw material and global commodity; grain traders (*sogo-shosha* in the case of Japan) to trade the oilseeds; first-stage food-processing industries to crush the soy into oil and meal; second-stage food-processing, feed, and livestock industries, as well as oleochemical and protein manufacturing, to produce a wide range of processed foods and non-food products; and mass-distribution by the supermarket, convenience store, and restaurant industries. The overview of its development and the related arguments are outlined in the Table C.1. In this way, the soy-industry provides much of the foundation of the "industrial mass diet" (Winson 2013), while also comprising a significant part of the "capitalist food system" (Holt-Giménez 2017).

DOI: 10.4324/9781032678733-7

The transformation of soy through mass-production and mass-distribution by "visible hands"

Soy was transformed into a versatile global commodity when modern big business began mass-production and mass-distribution of soy products. When the Japanese companies began the capitalist mode of production and established large-scale production capacity of mechanical-industry, it continuously required large-scale markets to sell its products to realize the value of its investment. The Japanese oil companies put enormous effort, over many decades, into increasing the usage of soy and soy products. In other words, soy was not intrinsically "versatile and cheap" (Prodöhl 2013), nor was it a miraculous or "magic bean" (Roth 2018) from the start; it was *made* versatile and cheap, and whatever magic or power soy may have has been the result of the power of capital.

After establishing themselves as a soy-meal-manufacturing industry and then losing the export markets for oil in the West, the Japanese soy-crushing companies set about creating domestic markets for soy oil and soy meal. They made huge capital investments in cutting-edge facilities and oleochemical technologies to expand the versatility of soy. They continued their research and development, production, and even some investment in new facilities during the wars under the control of the state and military. After WWII, when defeated Japan came under US hegemony, the Japanese oil companies collaborated with the governments of Japan and the United States to develop the markets for edible oils.

In Figure C.1, I depicted how the mass-production structure of modern big business requires large volumes of raw materials, thus impacting agricultural production; and how it requires more markets and mass-sales of its products, thus impacting consumers' diet.

In the case of the soy-industry with modernizing Japan, the key of this structure, I argue, was the shift of soy-crushing into the capitalist mode of production, which saw the mechanization of the industry for the mass-processing of soy at large-scale factories in the port districts, built with large capital investment in both machinery and technology. To utilize their production capacity, these factories needed a large volume of raw materials, which they supplied with imported soy, first from Manchuria, then from the United States, and later from Latin America. In order to meet the increased demand for raw materials from the processing industries, oil crop agriculture also became a large-scale industry and began mass-producing soy as cash crop and a global commodity, rather than as food for people. This process has been discussed as the capitalist appropriation of agriculture in previous research.

Table C.1 Overview of the soy-industry development and the related arguments in Chapters 2–5

	Ch. 2 Japan's modernization and imperial expansion (19th C to WWI)	*Ch. 3 Post-WWI recession and Japan's continued militarization and expansion in Asia (interwar period)*	*Ch. 4 The shift to edible oil and US soy after WWII (1940s–1950s)*	*Ch. 5 Increasing Japan's edible oil consumption (mid-1950s–1970s)*
Main theme	Development of Manchurian soy-industry and export of soy products (bean, meal, oil), as part of Japan's state-building project	Expanding soy's versatility in multiple markets for business survival and as a colonial strategy	Shift of resources from Asian oil crops to US soy Shift of markets from military supplies to food products	The supply side works to create increasing demand for soy oil and soy meal
Products and markets	Beginning of mass-production of soy meal and soy oil by capital-intensive mechanical-industry Meal: fertilizer for cash crops (to accumulate foreign capital) Oil: export commodity to Europe and the US	Soy (bean, oil, meal) and hardened soy oil become raw materials for industrial and military manufacturing: soy-based glue, plastic, paint, etc.; also a few food products (edible soy oil went on sale in the 1920s)	Soy becomes an important source of military materials (oil and protein as petroleum substitute), e.g., lubricant, aviation oil, biofuel, explosives ↓ Japan welcomes US soy and begins using soy to feed the hungry nation (edible oils, margarine, etc. go to food market)	The era of mass-production and mass-consumption of factory-made oil-rich food products Oil becomes an everyday food stuff: Edible soy oil, processed food products (made from imported grain and oilseeds), food services (esp. fast food)

Main companies involved	*Zaibatsu* with "government trader" sectors: Mitsui, Mitsubishi Soy-crushing companies: Nisshin Oil (with Okura), Honen Oil (with Suzuki Shoten) South Manchuria Railway (SMR)	Old and new *zaibatsu* form *Konzern*, invest in new oleochemical and military sectors: Nisshin Oil, Honen Oil, Ajinomoto, Kao Soap, Nippon Oil (linked to Suzuki Shoten, Nissan *Konzern*) South Manchuria Railway (SMR) research and lab sector	Dissolution of *zaibatsu*; traders become "general trading companies," i.e., *sogo-shosha* including Itochu, Marubeni; Mitsui and Mitsubishi soon reorganize Nisshin Oil, Honen Oil, Ajinomoto, Yoshihara Oil, Nippon Oil and other oleochemical manufacturers become edible oil and margarine suppliers	US government and its soy-industry ASA (American Soybean Association) Japanese government and its big food business in oil, flour, milk, feed, livestock companies *Sogo-shosha*: Mitsui, Mitsubishi, Itochu, Marubeni, Sojitz
The "visible hands" of business and government	*Zaibatsu*-invested big business and "government traders" and Japan's colonial agent, SMR: Their capital investment in powered machinery and new technologies, enabling mass-production of soy meal and oil SMR contributes to soy's global trade, facilitating a transport system, standardization, quality control, improvement of soy products as higher-quality global commodities	Big business with mass-production capacity needs to expand market to survive: R&D to increase versatility of soy oil and meal products Development of oleochemical and protein technologies SMR lab's mission to utilize Manchurian resources for Japan's benefit Competitive markets and economic depression encourage industry concentration, with capital investment from old and new *zaibatsu*	Oil and oleochemical industries designated "important war industries" for military supplies Big business continues R&D and production under military orders during war Resources from Japanese occupation of Asian regions and Manchukuo ↓ US-led occupation government manages oil-crop allocation and markets for the benefit of big business; Japanese oil companies with oversized production capacity welcome US soy	Japan/US governments and big business PR campaigns promote oil-rich foods and the "Westernization of diet" Development of food and livestock industries as big business *Sogo-shosha* lead integration of oil crop imports, oil and meal production, food-processing, intensive livestock industries, and food retail and restaurant services

(*Continued*)

Table C.1 (Continued)

	Ch. 2 Japan's modernization and imperial expansion (19th C to WWI)	*Ch. 3 Post-WWI recession and Japan's continued militarization and expansion in Asia (interwar period)*	*Ch. 4 The shift to edible oil and US soy after WWII (1940s–1950s)*	*Ch. 5 Increasing Japan's edible oil consumption (mid-1950s–1970s)*
The role of soy and oil in food and capitalist history	Soy-industry in and trade from Manchuria (soy meal to Japan, soy oil to the West, and soy bean to Japan and Europe) helped Japan accumulate capital for industrial development and expansion in Asia as part of Japan's state-building project The First Food Regime in the Asian context	The soy and oleochemical/protein industries integrated for military purposes as Japan builds its imperial and military power "Flexing" soy between the Food Regimes	Soy, rapeseed, castor, and other oil crops managed by the military-government, and oil-related industries consolidated into a wartime institution, to provide the supplies for Japan to wage wars ↓ US soy becomes a commodity to incorporate Japan into the Second Food Regime under US hegemony	Japan realizes rapid economic growth while making food and agriculture cheaper by increasing imports of grain and oil crops from North America; Japan copies US models and integrates into US soy-corn-animal complex and durable (processed) food complex in the Second Food Regime

Source: Produced by the author.

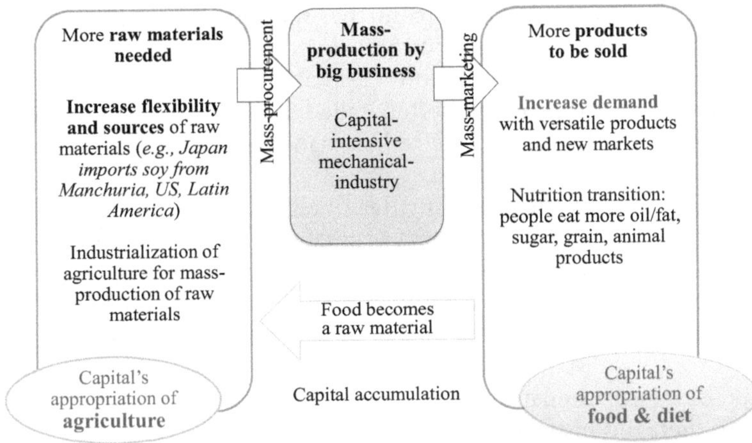

Figure C.1 How the soy mass-production structure actively transforms agriculture and food systems.

Source: Produced by the author.

The deep forests of Manchuria were cut down beginning in the 19th century to grow more soy for export, when Manchuria was connected to the world market by railways, including Japan's South Manchuria Railway. Manchuria became the world's largest source of soy exports by the 1930s. Then, the United States increased its soy cultivation, and it became a major producer and exporter of soy after WWII. In the 1970s, vast land in Latin America were "developed" to mass-produce soy. The process of soy cultivation impacting local society and environment has begun more than a century ago in Manchuria, long before globalization or neoliberal projects began in the 1980s.

Turning to the consumption side of Figure C.1, once the soy-industry had established as a capital-intensive mechanical-industry, it requires large-scale markets to sell its mass-produced soy products continuously. So the industry devoted great efforts to increasing the usage of soy meal and soy oil and developed a wide range of soy products for industrial, military, and food applications. The industry made soy into what the current academic discourse argues is the most prominent and established of the "flex crops," that is, crops that have "multiple uses (food, feed, fuel, fiber, industrial material, etc.) that can be flexibly interchanged while some consequent supply gaps can be filled by other flex crops" (Borras et al. 2016, 94). In addition to expanding the versatility of soy in multiple markets, the development of related industries, especially the processed food and intensive livestock industries, helped create larger volume demand for soy products, which, in turn, led the industry to further increase the supply. An oil-rich diet was promoted by government campaigns and some nutritional experts. In this way, the "nutrition transition" (Popkin 2002) to eating more oil and fat and more animal products, often called the "Westernization of diet," was promoted by the supply side rather than demanded by the consumers as part of a "natural" progression.

It is a common practice and a matter of course for businesses to develop new products and expand markets. Capitalism "can and must constantly accumulate, constantly search out new markets, constantly impose its imperatives on new territories and new spheres of life, on all human beings and the natural environment" (Wood 1999, 97). The issue is that, although we live in a capitalist food system, we tend to overlook its imperative of "competition, accumulation, and profit-maximization" when discussing food and diet, and instead blame the "usual suspects": consumer tastes and a "nutrition transition."

In this capitalist world-economy, soy and the related industries that developed along with the modernizing Japan survived a century of time by flexibly shifting their products and markets. The huge capital investment from *zaibatsu* and the collaborating works of their traders (later *sogo-shosha*) worked together, as well as Japanese government and its military and colonial institutions at some stages. These "visible hands" of big business and government actively intervened in, and promoted, the transformation of soy as they impacted agriculture and our diet. It was a common practice and a matter of course as a capitalist system. It should not be confused with natural development or people's demand only because soy is an agricultural crop and eaten as food.

Global food regimes and the formation of Japan's modern food system

Food issues are often regarded as issues of agricultural supply and consumer demand within a certain nation. In order to overcome this mindset, this book purposely focused on the business history of soy and positioned the development of the soy-industry in a global "food and capitalist history" (McMichael 2013), that is, within the Food Regime frameworks. The book thus illuminates how the modern soy- and oil-industries developed as Japan "regulated" its capital accumulation for their development, and how this process took place within the global Food Regimes, rather than just as a result of Japan's domestic agriculture and food issues.

Japan was a closed country for about two centuries in the feudal era (from the 1630s to the mid-19th century). During that isolation, the country was more or less self-sufficient in food, and its commerce and economy developed within its own borders. By the time Japan opened its markets in the mid-19th century, the global trade of wheat and sugar had been established around the Atlantic Ocean; this was the First Food Regime discussed by the previous literature (Friedmann and McMichael 1989 and others). Soon enough, Japan was importing wheat flour from the United States (it was literally called "American flour," *meriken-ko*, in Japan) and sugar as well. The Japanese *zaibatsu*, including Mitsui, Mitsubishi, and Suzuki Shoten, handled these international trade while developing their trading sectors. They were supported by the newly established Japanese government, and together they expanded into other parts of Asia. As part of this state-building project, the *zaibatsu* invested in the soy-crushing industry, mainly to produce soy meal for fertilizer. Increased import and production of soy meal, based on Manchurian soy, contributed to Japan's industrial revolution by providing the fertilizer input that enabled the country to increase its exports of silk products and to accumulate capital and keep it in Japanese hands. I argue that this incorporation of Manchurian soy into the structure of Japan's capital accumulation was the First Food Regime in the Asian context (Hiraga and Hisano 2017).

During the transitional period between the Food Regimes, the same large companies survived by reshaping soy into a flexible crop that could be used in many ways, mainly in non-food industries, including munitions manufacturing to wage wars. Then, after WWII, Japan became deeply embedded in the Second Food Regime under US hegemony. Japan was not a passive receiver of US soy and grains, however. On the contrary, this research reveals the active involvement of Japanese actors, who "copied" US models and worked to "integrate" the nation into the US grain and oilseed complexes: both the soy-corn-animal complex and the durable (processed) food complex. Japanese oil companies, which had built large-scale production capacity for soy products before and during the world wars, welcomed both US soy and the US-centered agri-food complexes. As a result, Japanese oil companies began to market large amounts of edible vegetable oils in Japan, and the Japanese large food and trading companies grew even larger on the basis of imported grain and oilseed. All of these processes have deeply impacted the Japanese diet.

In conclusion, I argue that the Japanese government and big business contributed significantly to transforming soy into a versatile global commodity beginning in the 19th century. The previous literature tends to consider how soy became a destructive political commodity in the recent decades of globalization or in neoliberal projects. As this book has demonstrated, however, soy had already been transformed, a century ago in Asia, even before it expanded beyond the region and was introduced to the Western world. Sure, soy used to be a wonderful traditional food that could be sustainably grown and was healthy for people. Such a soy is still possible but describes only a tiny fraction of the soy grown and used in today's world, both in the West and the East. The century-long development of the soy-industry and its global dissemination did little to advance the health and well-being of the population. It was rather a means for big business and governments to gain power along with capitalist development.

The key purpose of food and farming is, or should be, to advance the health and well-being of the population (Lang and Rayner 2002, 3–4). However, the current agriculture and food systems, including soy cultivation and the soy-industry, are criticized as destructive systems responsible for the ill-being of the population and the global climate crisis. This situation is not because the systems are broken; on the contrary, they are working very well, as capitalist food systems are supposed to, to accumulate capital while exploiting society and the environment, as Holt-Giménez (2017) argues. Further research is being conducted by many scholars on the current relation of soy with progressing inequality and the climate crisis, as well as the shift of powerful players of the soy-industry to Latin America and China, and now to Africa. I hope this book's business history of soy entwined with modernizing Japan sheds new light on the fundamental understanding and the underlying logic surrounding soy's transformation that applies to current issues as well.

Bibliography

In English

Borras Jr, S. M., Franco, J. C., Isakson, S. R., Levidow, L., and Vervest, P. (2016) "The Rise of Flex Crops and Commodities: Implications for Research", *The Journal of Peasant Studies*, 43(1), pp. 93–115.

Friedmann, H. and McMichael, P. (1989) "Agriculture and the State System: The Rise and Decline of National Agricultures, 1870 to the Present", *Sociologia Ruralis*, 29(2), pp. 93–117.

Hiraga, M. and Hisano, S. (2017) "The First Food Regime in Asian Context? Japan's Capitalist Development and the Making of Soybean as a Global Commodity in the 1890s-1930s", *AGST Working Paper Series* No. 2017-3, Asian Platform for Global Sustainability & Transcultural Studies (Japan Gateway Program), Kyoto University.

Holt-Giménez, E. (2017) *A Foodie's Guide to Capitalism: Understanding the Political Economy of What We Eat*, Monthly Review Press.

Lang, T. and Rayner, G. eds. (2002) *Why Health Is the Key to the Future of Food and Farming: A Report on the Future of Farming and Food*, Thames Valley University.

McMichael, P. (2013) *Food Regimes and Agrarian Questions*, Fernwood Publishing.

Popkin, B. (2002) 'The Dynamics of the Dietary Transition in the Developing World', in Caballero, B. and Popkin, B., (eds.), *The Nutrition Transition: Diet and Disease in the Developing World, Food Science and Technology International Series* (pp. 111–128), Academic Press.
Prodöhl, I. (2013) "Versatile and Cheap: A Global History of Soy in the First Half of the Twentieth Century", *Journal of Historical Geography*, 8(3), pp. 461–482.
Roth, M. (2018). *Magic Bean: The Rise of Soy in America*, University Press of Kansas.
Winson, A. (2013) *The Industrial Diet: The Degradation of Food and the Struggle for Healthy Eating*, New York University Press.
Wood, E. M. (1999) *The Origin of Capitalism*, Monthly Review Press.

Appendix

The basic information for the main companies discussed in this book

(Their representative name used in this book; their current name and the website. They all have English pages on their website, but I list the URL for their top page to avoid the broken link in future).

- **Mitsui**
  Mitsui & Co., Ltd. (三井物産株式会社)
  www.mitsui.com
- **Mitsubishi**
  Mitsubishi Corporation (三菱商事株式会社)
  www.mitsubishicorp.com

Note: These are *sogo-shosha*, general trading companies, today, though Mitsui and Mitsubishi also indicate the name of *zaibatsu* and wider corporate groups.

- **Nisshin Oil**
  The Nisshin OilliO Group, Ltd. (日清オイリオグループ株式会社)
  www.nisshin-oillio.com
- **Honen Oil**
  J-Oil Mills, Inc. (株式会社J-オイルミルズ)
  www.j-oil.com
- **Ajinomoto**
  Ajinomoto Co., Inc. (味の素株式会社)
  www.ajinomoto.com/

Note: The main edible oil companies today. Honen Oil, Ajinomoto's oil subsidiary, and Yoshihara Oil consolidated and became J-Oil Mills of today. Ajinomoto Co. supplies much wider food products than edible oil and oil products.

Nippon Oil & Fats
NOF Corporation (日油株式会社)
www.nof.co.jp

Kao Soap
Kao Corporation (花王株式会社)
www.kao.com

A postscript

There once was a time, before I began my academic career, that I promoted handmade biodiesel made from waste cooking oil. The project leader at the time, Keith Addison, wrote, on our first attempt at fuel making, as follows:

> We turned our kitchen into a sort of illicit still and made a hell of a mess in there brewing biodiesel fuel out of about 60 litres of yukky waste cooking oil we got from behind McDonald's one night (they were happy to give it to us once we told them we didn't want to eat it). We were sure it would work, but we had to try it ourselves first—we're not chemists, and if we can make it anyone can. And it works! Amazing! Last night we put the stuff in Midori's old diesel Land Rover and it ran like a dream and smelt like a bunch of roses! Well, French fried roses anyway. Now it runs clean, on waste Big Mac residues we brewed up in a bucket in the kitchen, and we're very tickled!
>
> (Email to *Journey to Forever* friends, Friday April 23, 1999: https://journeytoforever.org/biodiesel.html)

After getting my hands greasy and smelling rotten cooking oils for about a decade, I already knew that there was a paper-thin difference between edible oils and petrol oil, and that they could easily substitute for each other; no matter if they are bio-origin or petrol-origin, oil and fat can be raw materials or energy for so many things. Then, after a decade of struggle, I gave up the heavy burden of this unfunded project. I shifted to academia, and went alone to City University London for a master's course on food policy. I believe the Centre for Food Policy is the research institute that studies food from the widest angle in the world, yet I never met anyone who researched vegetable oils in our diet. To my surprise, vegetable oil had very little attention among the leading social science scholars on agriculture and food, and it was too little researched compared to sugar or animal products. A presentation of mine on vegetable oil was once categorized in a "shapeless food" session (along with Jell-O) at a meeting of an academic association for food studies. The situation was worse when I came back to Japan; edible oil was not even considered as food but categorized as a seasoning, and a respected senior scholar once criticized me for applying Food Regime frameworks on soy oil. Yet, most people eat vegetable oil almost every day, in both the West and the East. In particular, soy, palm, and rapeseed/canola oils have tremendous impacts on so many people's daily diet in this world, even though their proliferation has a surprisingly short history, emerging as they did with modernization. The more I study, the more I find that the greasy, dirty, disgusting issues of colonization and wars, exploitation and destruction, and drastic impacts on us and the environment are related to vegetable oils just as they are to petrol oils. This is why I began studying the political economy of provisioning vegetable oils in industrial mass diet.

I titled my master's thesis, which I submitted to City University London in 2012, "How Does Trade Liberalisation Facilitate Nutrition Transition? Examples of Structural Changes in China and India's Vegetable Oil and Animal Feed Supply Chains and Their Dietary Impact." In those days, China and India were the leading importers of soy and palm oil. Then, when I came back to Japan and began studying how vegetable oils became popular among Japanese people, I soon found myself dragged into the forests of Manchuria, the colonization projects of Imperial Japan, battles in Asia and the Pacific, and the accumulated literature on *zaibatsu* and capitalist history. As I took dusty classified wartime reports from the underground bookshelves of the ex-imperial Kyoto University library, I wondered why I needed to research Japanese colonial institutions and *zaibatsu* when I wanted to study food and diets. But there was no avoiding it: The imperial and military government and big business were the most significant players in the rise of edible oils and in shaping modern food systems in Japan, as this book has demonstrated. I found that soy and vegetable oils can be good research topics to understand food and capitalist history. So here I am.

This book is based on my PhD project ("The Transformation of Food with Capitalist Development: The Development Trajectory of Vegetable Oil Supply System in Japan"), which I submitted to the Graduate School of Economics of Kyoto University in 2018. I published it as a Japanese book in 2019, with the title *The Political Economy of Vegetable Oils: The Capitalist Food System Studied from the Perspective of Soy and Oils*. To publish this work in English, however, I significantly changed its theoretical frameworks, shifting the focus from agri-food research toward business and capitalist history. Thus, it became a business history of soy.

I believe the case of Japan offers a vivid demonstration of the political economy of the proliferation of vegetable oils in our daily diet, and not only because I am Japanese. One reason is that, because the Japanese people had little habit of eating fats, the introduction of vegetable oils was extremely visible, requiring new products and new cooking methods, unlike in the Western diet, where vegetable oil products like margarine and shortenings gradually replaced commonly used animal fat products, such as butter and lard. Another reason is that modernizing Japan had to procure soy and rapeseed from overseas (mainly from the Asian continent), and those that handled these trade items were very big players indeed, including imperial, colonial, and military institutions, together with the *zaibatsu* and the South Manchuria Railway. Their historical materials recorded their activities around Manchurian soy, although they were fragmented, with less attention paid to these resources compared to coal or steel. By gathering these fragmented descriptions in old books and dusted papers, I was able to compile this historical development of soy and oil. My previous hands-on experience with biodiesel and used cooking oils also helped, of course. Because of that previous experience, I had no assumptions regarding vegetable oils as food per se, contrary to many people's understanding of edible oils as essential for the human diet.

Some of my earlier writings that partially deal with the topics of this book have been published in English:

Hiraga, M., and Hisano, S. (2017). "The first Food Regime in Asian context? Japan's capitalist development and the making of soybean as a global commodity in the 1890s–1930s" (*AGST Working Paper Series No. 2017-03*). Kyoto: Asian Platform for Global Sustainability & Transcultural Studies.

Hiraga, M. (2018). "Financialization in Japanese agri-food regimes: Uncovering the role of *sogo-shosha* in global soy investment", in Bjorkhaug, H., Magnan, A. and Lawrence, G. eds. *The Financialization of Agri-Food Systems: Contested Transformations*, Routledge, pp. 156–175.

I have also presented parts of this research at various academic conferences and in their proceedings. Nevertheless, this book is the first publication that presents a comprehensive business history of soy and modernizing Japan for English readers.

So many people have guided me and supported me to this point. I'd like to thank HISANO Shuji and OKADA Tomohiro, my PhD supervisors in the Graduate School of Economics of Kyoto University; KUROSAWA Takafumi and Matthias Kipping, who introduced me to the world of business history; HISANO Ai and other series editors of Routledge International Studies in Business History, who supported me in my long struggle of writing my first book proposal. I also thank Laurie Durand, who corrected my manuscript to become more readable English.

I also want to thank the agri-food scholars who advised me in my research, especially those in the Research Committee of the Sociology of Agriculture and Food in the International Sociological Association (RC40 ISA) and the Agri-Food Research Network. Harriet Friedmann and Philip McMichael gave me advice by attending the Food Regime session that I organized in ISA 2018, and Hugh Campbell, Geoffrey Lawrence, Bill Pritchard, and many agri-food scholars took notice on my research and encouraged me from the early stage. Tim Lang and the scholars at the Centre for Food Policy at the City University London gave me my first training in food-related research. I appreciate the institutional support from Kyoto University, Ritsumeikan University, and Kyoto Tachibana University, where I passed my graduate school days, conducted postdoctoral work, and am currently affiliated. Thanks to my researcher friends in the weekly online writeshop for their encouragement and comments, which are precious in this somewhat lonely research environment in Japan.

My sincere appreciation goes to many people in civil society around Kyoto who work in food and agriculture; in food banks, organic movements, agroecology, as well as on issues of globalization and municipalism.

Finally, but not least, thanks to my ex-partner and project leader, the late Keith Addison, who taught me more than anyone else about this world, and with whom I shared a decade of my life. Another decade has passed since his death, and I finally have managed to publish this book, dedicating it to him with my deepest appreciation.

Index

Note: Endnotes are indicated by the page number followed by "n" and the note number e.g., 111n5 refers to note 5 on page 111.

Kolibri 360 GmbH
Ferdinand-Jühlke-Straße 7
99095 Erfurt, Deutschland
produktsicherheit@kolibri360.de